# EVALUATING EMPLOYEE ASSISTANCE PROGRAMS

# EVALUATING EMPLOYEE ASSISTANCE PROGRAMS:

## A SOURCEBOOK FOR THE ADMINISTRATOR AND COUNSELOR

by
JERRY SPICER
WITH
PATRICIA OWEN
AND
DAVID LEVINE

First published, June, 1983.

© 1983 Hazelden Foundation. All rights reserved. No portion of this book may be reproduced without the written permission of the publisher.

ISBN: 0-89486-180-8

Printed in the United States of America.

# ACKNOWLEDGMENTS

Major funding for this report came from the Minnesota Mining and Manufacturing (3M) Company, and we would like to thank 3M and Ed Scharlau, 3M's Employee Assistance Manager, for their help in providing direction and support for the project. Other employers, including the InterNorth Company, Continental Telephone, and Hennepin County encouraged us in our evaluation efforts and allowed us to report the data from studies of their programs. Without the guidance and assistance of people working directly in the field we would not have been able to complete this project and address what are major evaluation needs for employee assistance programs. We interviewed members of the Minnesota Association for Employee Assistance Program Administrators and Counselors (MEAPAC), and the Association of Labor/Management Counselors and Administrators groups in Washington D.C. and California, and talked with numerous other professionals in the field. These individuals were all helpful, and we hope that this report will enable them to provide better services for their employees.

Finally, we would like to thank the staff of Hazelden's Evaluation and Employee Assistance Services departments, in particular Don Jones and Tim Plant, for their work in designing many of the studies discussed in this paper and assisting us in the preparation of this manuscript. Several other authors, notably Attkisson, Hayward, Erfurt, Foote, Roman, Schramm, Schlenger and Trice have written extensively in this area and we acknowledge their work. We apologize for any misinterpretations, which are our errors. No doubt we have missed some studies and newer research, an unavoidable problem in a rapidly expanding field.

# CONTENTS

| | Page |
|---|---|
| PREFACE | ix |
| Purpose of the Study | ix |
| Overview of the Text | x |

**Chapter One** — WHAT IS EVALUATION? 3
  Evaluation as a Management Tool 3
  Process and Impact Studies 4
  Special Issues in Evaluating EAPs 5
    The Diversity of Program Models 6
    The Problem of Goals 10
    The Lack of Previous Research 12
    Basics in Designing a Useful Evaluation 14

**Chapter Two** — HOW TO EVALUATE EAPs 16
  An Overview of Research Methods 16
    Data Collection Options 16
    Three Important Methodological Issues 17
      Choosing the Criteria 17
      Choosing the Sample 18
      Analyzing the Data 21
  Needs Assessment Studies 26
  Process Evaluation 27
    Studies of Program Implementation 27
    Characteristics of Troubled Employees 30
    Records and Information Systems 32
    Training Evaluation 37
    Evaluating External Resources 39

Impact Evaluation 47
  Suggestions for Conducting Follow-up Studies 47
  Outcomes of Employer Referrals to Hazelden 49
  Follow-up Study of EAP Clients 54
  Other Studies of Client Outcome 56
  Employee Surveys 58
  Client Satisfaction Studies: Findings 58
  Cost-Benefit Studies: Findings 60
  Cost-Effectiveness Analysis: An Alternative to Cost-Benefit 64

CONCLUSIONS
  What Do We Know About Broadbrush EAPs? 68
  Recommendations For Further Research 69
  Making Evaluation Usable 71

REFERENCES 74

APPENDICES 79
  One — An Overview of Research Methods 81
  Two — Summaries of Selected Studies 93

# PREFACE

## PURPOSE OF THE STUDY

Although Employee Assistance Programs (EAPs) may have been first developed in the 1940's, it has been the 1970's that have seen the major growth in employer-based services. However, the growth in services has not been accompanied by an increase in evaluation. Although there have been several major studies of alcohol-focused employee assistance programs, there are very little data on the broadbrush model. It is our intention in this paper to discuss not only what has been done in the area of evaluation of employee assistance programs, but more importantly, to talk about new directions and new methods. Throughout the book we have tried to include samples of instruments and discussions of other studies in order to help the reader better understand evaluation. Our goal is to help fill the gap between increasing accountability demands for employee assistance programs and a lack of skills in evaluation abilities in the field. Our objective was not to write a highly sophisticated research monograph directed at the academic researcher. Rather, our interest is to provide persons working in the employee assistance field with the tools and knowledge so that they can better evaluate and manage their programs. We have tried to strike a middle ground by focusing on the person who has some background in using data and who is familiar with employee assistance programs. In many cases the evaluation strategies discussed here could more appropriately be called monitoring and documentation rather than evaluation research. However, because most employee assistance programs are not collecting and using data there is a need for the first level of program evaluation. We have included in the appendix a special section on research methodology for the person who needs some assistance in this area.

## OVERVIEW OF THE TEXT

In the next section we discuss what evaluation is and special issues in evaluating EAPs. Chapter Two will present specific evaluation techniques ranging from needs assessments to cost-benefit studies. The conclusions will be followed by a technical appendix on research methods and a synopsis of selected published research. This sourcebook has been written so that the reader may concentrate on certain chapters or skip to other areas. References are included for the person who wishes more information. In many cases we have referred to studies done at Hazelden, not as models of what other programs should do, but as examples of successful and not-so-successful projects. As we reviewed the methodological problems of other studies we found that we too had made similar mistakes, but even though the methods often varied, many researchers in the field have found similar results. Unfortunately, much of the unpublished research we reviewed was not for general release, but we do appreciate the willingness of other programs to share data with us.

Another publication, *Performance Benchmarks for the Comprehensive Employee Assistance Program*,* summarizes data from Hazelden's EAP research and is recommended as a companion piece to the more general report.

---

*\*Performance Benchmarks for the Comprehensive Employee Assistance Program*, Donald R. Jones, Hazelden Educational Materials, Center City, MN 1983.

# Chapter One

## WHAT IS EVALUATION?

### EVALUATION AS A MANAGEMENT TOOL

To evaluate means to make a judgment about the value of something. As used in this paper, evaluation means the process of collecting empirical, objective information to enable us to better judge the efficiency and effectiveness of employee assistance services. Our perspective is that evaluation should be a management tool. As Attkisson (1978:22) says, "Evaluation is primarily a process within ongoing organization, decision-making, and planning; and it is only secondarily a research enterprise for the purpose of new scientific discoveries." Although more theoretical research with employee assistance programs is clearly warranted, we are less concerned at this point with theoretical issues and more concerned with the use of empirical evaluative data in program management and decision-making. It is our feeling that the well-run employee assistance program of the future will, of necessity, be required to have a cost-effective and useful evaluation system built into the program.

Another way of looking at evaluation is to consider what evaluation is not designed to accomplish. As indicated above, evaluation is not the same as pure research. Evaluative data are part of a decision-making process that includes a variety of factors that directly affect the values that we have concerning employees and their problems. Evaluation is often threatening to people, and persons conducting an evaluation study must be careful to consider organizational dynamics early in the planning process. Evaluation will not provide "proof" or the final answer to problems with an employee assistance program. "In the balance, one can only expect reasonable judgments and not scientifically verified facts." (Attkisson, 1978:24.) Evaluation is constrained by factors of time and money, and in the work place, issues of confidentiality and access to employees limit the sophistication of the research design. What is important for the evaluator to know is how to conduct sound applied research that results in reliable data. We believe that this type of evaluation *is* possible with EAPs, and we will indicate strengths and weaknesses of various evaluation tools in later sections.

## PROCESS AND IMPACT STUDIES

Michael Patton (1978:26) defines evaluation research as, "The systematic collection of information about the activities and outcomes of actual programs in order for interested persons to make judgments about specific aspects of what the program is doing and affecting." In this definition Patton raises several significant points about evaluation. First of all, evaluation is systematic. That is, evaluation is something that is done in a planned, organized manner with the objective of providing information to key decisionmakers. Evaluation does not limit itself only to what the program is doing, but also studies program effects and impact. This is what evaluators have called process and outcome or impact evaluation. When we are interested in studying what the program is doing we are asking essentially *process questions*. In the employee assistance field, typical process issues would be how many clients are seen in a certain time period, the types of problems employees have when they contact the program, the referral rate, etc. On the other hand, *outcome questions* take a look at the program's impact. Typical impact issues for the employee assistance field would be job performance changes, cost-benefit, client satisfaction, and client outcome. Throughout the text we will be referring to types of evaluations the administrator can use to address both process and impact questions.

But again, our audience is not the professional evaluator welltrained in research techniques, but the program staff more interested in internal developmental studies. We do recommend that all EAPs utilize professional evaluation expertise when needed and periodically be assessed by an external, objective evaluator (Roman, 1981). The evaluation team should include both internal staff and external help, particularly if the objectivity of internal persons is likely to be questioned.

## SPECIAL ISSUES IN EVALUATING EAPS

Most of the usual evaluation methodologies can be used in studying EAPs, but there are some unique aspects of these programs that need to be considered. By surveying and interviewing other EAP professionals, we found several major evaluation needs and problems. Table 1 summarizes the results of over 100 interviews and mailed questionnaire returns from a non-random "interested person" survey. The surveys and our literature review found six major factors affecting EAP evaluation:

1. There is a great variation in program models (Phillips and Older, 1981) complicating the development of standardized evaluation tools.

2. So little research has been done that we lack any benchmarks or standards of success. Furthermore, too many studies have been done that do not meet minimal research standards.

3. Organizational dynamics and concerns with employee confidentiality limit access to data.

4. Many EAPs are changing from an informal entrepreneurial model to a formal structure and have yet to establish measurable goals and objectives.

5. EAPs have many constituencies (Roman, 1980), each with its own unique evaluation goals.

6. The majority of EAP professionals do not have evaluation expertise.

Each of these factors can be summarized into three topics of (1) program models, (2) goal-setting problems, and (3) the lack of previous research.

## Table 1
## MAJOR EVALUATION NEEDS AND PROBLEMS, ACCORDING TO EAP PROFESSIONALS*

Evaluation Priorities In Rank Order:
1. Assessing the quality of referral sources (first priority)
2. Client outcome
3. Client satisfaction
4. Employee awareness
5. Program utilization/penetration
6. Job performance changes
7. Supervisory attitudes
8. Cost-benefit
9. Training effectiveness
10. Effectiveness of written materials

Barriers To EAP Evaluation, In Rank Order:
1. Insufficient time
2. Union/management relationships
3. Lack of money
4. Reliability and accuracy of employee records
5. Access to cost data
6. Access to employee records
7. Lack of expertise
8. Management attitudes
9. Employee attitudes
10. Staff attitudes

*These are the responses of EAP counselors and administrators; no doubt management, unions, etc. would have different priorities (see Table 2).

## The Diversity of Employee Assistance Program Models

EAPs vary according to several dimensions, at least three of which are: (1) whether the focus is on alcohol, all problems (the broadbrush model), or wellness; (2) whether the program is an internal or external service, and (3) whether the program is formally or informally managed.

For example, an internally located informal alcohol-only program would be the recovered alcoholic who informally intervenes for employees with evident alcohol problems and may refer the employee to Alcoholics Anonymous following a discussion over lunch. The other extreme would be the external broadbrush program which relies on employee training and written communications, and depends on supervisory referrals to academically trained counselors. These professionals are familiar with a broad range of human services and keep extensive documentation on the clients.

These dimensions can also be understood by asking the following questions:

1. *What problem areas are handled by the EAP?* Programs for employees fall into one of the following categories:

   a. *Alcohol-only programs* — dealing with problems related to alcohol and drug use.

   b. *Broadbrush programs* — dealing with all problems, e.g., emotional/psychological problems, marital and family problems, job stress, alcohol and drug problems, legal problems, financial problems.

   c. *Wellness programs* — dealing with health promotion in general, and advocate anticipation and prevention of all problems as well as the treatment of them (Curran and Kiefhaber, 1980).

The trend appears to be away from alcohol-only programs toward broadbrush programs (US. Department of Health, Education & Welfare, 4th Special Report) and there is also growth in health-promotion and wellness programs. Edwards (1975) describes the history of EAPs and relates the trend toward broadbrush programs as being parallel to the growth of community mental health centers in America. A main benefit Edwards describes is that broadbrush programs may actually be more successful in reaching employees with alcohol problems because (1) the stigma of seeking help for alcoholism may be reduced, (2) broadbrush programs may help prevent alcohol problems before drinking problems reach a chronic stage, and (3) employees may seek help for problems they perceive as *not* alcohol-related, when in fact, alcohol use is a major problem. In the latter case, it may be that the

EAP counselor perceives and redefines the employee's problem during the initial interviews. Studies of broadbrush EAPs support this idea; when clients' perceptions of the problem were compared with counselors' perceptions, counselors were much more likely than clients to perceive alcohol as the problem (Foote, Erfurt, Strach, & Guzzardo, 1978; Plant, 1981).

2. *How formal is the program?* This dimension of EAP models is actually a continuum with very formal programs at one end and very informal programs at the other. "Formality" includes the following aspects of EAP programs:

*How was the organization's EAP established?* An example of a formal model is an EAP that is built on recommendations from meetings between union and management representatives. At the other extreme (informality), the policy toward troubled employees may be decided by one recovering alcoholic employee who, on his or her own, attempts to identify and help problem drinking co-workers.

*How are troubled employees identified?* In a formal program, supervisors are provided with training sessions to teach them how to identify and refer workers with lowered levels of job performance. Use of videotapes and/or role-playing may be used as teaching methods. In informal programs, identification of troubled employees may depend on the intuition and interest of supervisors and co-workers.

*How are the employees made aware of the organization's employee assistance program?* In a formal program, employees may be oriented through meetings, notices in organization newsletters, postings on bulletin boards, and brochures sent to their homes. In an informal program, employees learn about the EAP primarily through word of mouth.

*What kinds of records are kept on employees who use EAPs?* In formal programs, a system of record keeping may include documentation of (1) client's background (demographic information, occupational history, referral information, treatment history, problem areas, occupational problems); (2) services record (number and nature of contacts with EAP);

(3) client follow-up (problem resolution, job performance changes, client satisfaction); (4) supervisor's reports (records of supervisory ratings before and after employee's contact with EAP); (5) cost-benefit data (dollar amounts saved and spent in rehabilitating troubled employees). In informal programs, few or no records may be kept.

3. *Where is the EAP located?* This third dimension of basic EAP models reflects another source of variability that affects both the operation and the evaluation of the EAP. Some employers have "in-house" EAP programs with services provided through the personnel or medical department or in a separate EAP division. Other employers may contract with an outside agency, paying them for counseling and referral services provided to their employees. A third alternative is a "consortium model" where several small organizations combine their funds and needs to provide one EAP for employees in all the organizations. In each of these locations, the organizational flow between management and the actual operation of the EAP may vary (Schramm, Mandell, and Archer, 1978, pp. 30–31). The variations in location of an EAP affect evaluation procedures. The accessibility of data and types of data available are particular to the location, as are the characteristics of the employees studied. And, the goals of the evaluation may differ accordingly.

As can be gathered from the above descriptions, there is no single EAP model. Instead, EAP models vary greatly in what services are offered (alcohol-only, broadbrush, or wellness), how employees are provided the services (formality), and where they go to get the services (location). It is also important to recognize that *often the theoretical EAP model that an organization chooses may differ considerably from how the EAP actually operates.* For example, while an organization may theoretically promote supervisory referrals based on documented lowered work performance, actual referrals to the organization's EAP may more often be a result of self-referrals or supervisors' intuition. In understanding or evaluating employee assistance programs, it is important to recognize any discrepancies between an organization's theoretical EAP model and the actual working model. Also, the *type of model or philosophy will affect the evaluation needs and capabilities of the EAP.* Before an evaluation study is begun, the program staff should carefully define the program model as it actually functions and design the evaluation to fit the reality of the EAP's philosophy and goals. A useful exercise is to define the program model by developing measurable goals, our next topic.

## The Problem of Goals

Employee assistance programs often differ in their goals because employers have various reasons for establishing EAPs. Curran and Kiefhaber (1980) cite four possible motivating factors: (1) "selfish altruism" — the belief that rehabilitating employees saves employers money in the long run; (2) recognition of legal responsibilities an employer may have for employees' mental health; (3) the increasing awareness and acceptance of mental illness in America, and (4) an increasing focus on employees' job performance rather than on personal problems. *EAPs developed with different purposes in mind will have different goals and definitions of success.* Careful thought and discussions with key people will be necessary to clearly define what the evaluation should seek to demonstrate — dollar savings, happier employees, healthier employees, etc. *An EAP may have multiple goals, and no single study will measure impact in all areas.* A first step in evaluation planning is to set priorities.

Because groups have different goals, they may also have different perspectives on accountability. The program consultant is concerned if the program is successfully implemented, the trainer if the employees understand how to use the EAP, and the counselor if the client follows through on the referrals. Ultimately, the basic question concerns the client's improvement, but a mix of evaluation methods must be used to demonstrate that each member of the EAP team is effective.

A related problem with goals is that they are often vague and unmeasureable. How *much* money should be saved? How *many* troubled employees should improve? These are the kinds of questions a goal-oriented evaluator will ask, and caution should be taken in not promising what cannot be delivered. Because there are so little data, we are faced with setting goals in a vacuum. As more studies are done, there will be more data giving us the ability to establish objective, realistic criteria. Evaluation can then be used to help determine goals, not simply to tell us we have succeeded or failed.

Another question is, "Whose goals are we evaluating?" The company president will have different goals than the union representative. *Before* the study begins, it must be determined whom the study is for. That person's questions need to be answered, but it should be recognized that not all constituencies will be satisfied with the same data (Roman, 1980). However, once one group's questions are answered, the evaluator will move into new areas and begin answering other questions. Table 2 illustrates different goals that various persons involved in the EAP might have, and Chapter Two will discuss alternatives for answering questions.

A final point on goals is that goal-oriented evaluation can be limiting in truly assessing all program impacts. A program usually has unintended positive *and* negative effects, and by studying only goal attainment, we can blind ourselves to these other effects. Again, evaluation should examine what we do and the effects we have in a broad sense, not only the three or four stated goals of the program.

**Table 2**

| Group: | Possible Evaluation Questions: |
|---|---|
| Top Management | Is the program cost-effective? Does it increase our productivity? What proportion of our employees are using the program? What main problem areas are common in our organization? Does the EAP help prevent accidents, absenteeism, etc.? |
| Employees using EAP | Are the services helpful? Are clients treated with respect and courtesy? Are my contacts with EAP kept confidential? Is the location convenient and appropriate? |
| Supervisors | Are the EAP services available when I need them? Does an employee's job performance improve after using the EAP? Will the EAP make my job easier? |

**Table 2** (continued)

| | |
|---|---|
| The EAP administrator or counselor | What types of problems do employees bring to us? Are we making helpful and appropriate assessments and referrals? Are we effective in helping employees maintain or improve their work performance? Are employees satisfied with our service? |
| Unions | Does the EAP provide an alternative to dismissing an employee? How will this program affect grievance and arbitration procedures? Is there a penalty for the employees using the EAP? |

(Adapted from discussions by Schramm et al. 1978)

## The Lack of Previous Research

The final issue centers around problems in methodology and research design. Because so few studies on the broadbrush model have been published, there is little solid data that can be used to support general statements about EAPs and employees who use them. Studies using good methodological principles (i.e., Schramm et al., 1978; Foote et al., 1978; Cole & Shupe, 1970) need further cross-validation before their findings can be stated with confidence. In spite of these problems, it is common in EAP literature to read rather surprising statements based more on interesting assumptions than on fact. Other reviewers have also pointed out this problem. The following list describes commonly held assumptions (with references given to reviewers who have discussed them):

1. *Assumption*: Early detection/intervention provides a better chance for recovery (this assumption is usually made regarding alcoholism, rather than other problems).

*Problems*: What are the criteria for detecting early alcoholism? Can we differentiate early alcoholism from alcohol abuse? What portion of these early alcoholics is likely to improve on their own, without treatment (i.e., "spontaneous remissions")? Are the same methods of intervention and treatment appropriate for beginning alcoholics and chronic or late-stage alcoholics? (see also Roman, 1980; Trice, 1980).

2. *Assumption*: Troubled employees can be detected by decreased work performance. Most EAP policies recommend that supervisors refer on the basis of lowered work performance, not on personal knowledge about the employee.

*Problems:* Are work performance criteria senstive enough to detect problems other than late-stage alcoholism? How many alcoholics/troubled employees actually manifest their problems through documentable behavior? (see also Googins and Kurtz, 1981).

3. *Assumption*: Supervisory confrontation works.

*Problems*: What proportion of supervisors avoid or use this method of helping troubled employees? What proportion of employees accept or reject the referral? Is confrontation beneficial for troubled employees without alcohol problems? (see also Googins & Kurtz, 1981).

4. *Assumption*: Improved work performance equals good outcome.

*Problems*: Are work performance indices sensitive enough to detect good or bad outcomes of intervention/treatment? What about employees whose work performance prior to intervention was adequate? (see Roman, 1980).

5. *Assumption*: Troubled employees need help.

*Problems*: What proportion of troubled employees improve without formal intervention/treatment (spontaneous remissions)? Are there less formal methods that may help a troubled employee? (see also Edwards, 1975).

6. *Assumption*: All eligible employees are equally likely to use an EAP.

*Problems*: Some workers' problems may be less obvious than others (e.g., white collar workers, independent workers, etc.). High level employees who can afford private therapy may avoid the company EAP. What effects do differential use patterns have on EAP utilization/penetration rates?

7. *Assumption*: Cost-benefit analysis is a good measure of EAP effectiveness.

*Problems*: To what extent can improvement among troubled employees be reflected in economic terms? Are most employers primarily interested in the economic gains from helping their employees? Can true financial benefits to an employer be measured in a relatively brief time frame (as is done in most studies)? Are the same cost-benefit formulas appropriate for all clients, regardless of the type of problem, job status, and seniority? (see also Foote, et al., 1978; Schramm, 1980).

8. *Assumption*: All EAPs need evaluation.

*Problems*: What are the goals of those involved with the EAP? How formal is the program (i.e., how available are the necessary data)? Is it feasible to do a good evaluation? An evaluation based on unrepresentative samples and vague criteria is *not* better than no evaluation at all.

The above list of assumptions frequently made about EAPs and evaluation of them is not exhaustive. Further, it is not intended to discourage advocates and evaluators of EAPs. On the contrary, awareness of these assumptions can provide the evaluator with questions that the evaluator should study. More specifically, there were also methodological weaknesses common in many of the studies we reviewed, but there is also a recent increase in interest and discussions of EAP evaluation (e.g., Foote and Erfurt, 1981; Roman, 1981). These will be discussed in Chapter Two.

## BASICS IN DESIGNING A USEFUL EVALUATION

Faced with all these programmatic and methodological problems, how can an evaluation study be implemented that will meet the required needs for reliable objective data? First of all, it is important to *know what evaluation can do*. Evaluation will not prove that the EAP is 100% effective. Evaluation is not promotion or marketing. Issues of accessibility of data and employee confidentiality will limit the ability to study certain areas. Secondly, *decide whom the study is for and what they need to know*. Don't promise everyone everything. Next, *plan the evaluation*. "How much time and money do you have?" and most importantly, "When will the report be due?" are questions that should be answered before the study starts. *Get help if you need it* is our next recommendation. Look for evaluation and research consultants who know EAPs, have experience, and can train you to take over the study. See if other EAP professionals can share and help. Finally, *make (and get) a commitment for developing systematic multi-focused evaluation*. Begin simply and plan on adding other studies as the program matures, but don't continue to do the same thing forever. Plan for an external, summative evaluation every two or three years. An advantage you will have is that evaluative research has rapidly developed in the last few years, and there are a number of methods that can be used, many of which are discussed next.

# Chapter Two

# HOW TO EVALUATE EAPs

Table 3 summarizes three basic types of evaluation, and the methods that can be used to answer the evaluation questions. The first type of evaluation is the *needs assessment* study that collects data before the program is implemented. *Process evaluation* options include information and records systems and evaluation of training and communications. *Impact evaluation* addresses issues of changes in employees' attitudes, problems, and job performance following implementation of the EAP.

Each of these approaches will be discussed in this chapter. Previous research, primarily of alcohol programs, will be summarized, followed by samples of instruments and results of Hazelden studies. But, before we describe the various approaches, we will briefly outline some key points about research methods.

## AN OVERVIEW OF RESEARCH METHODS

### Data Collection Options

Evaluation data can be collected in four basic ways — by using *records* or standardized *reporting forms*, by *surveys* (mail or telephone), by *interviews*, and from *observation*. We will not discuss observational approaches here, but Patton (1980) has written an excellent book describing the use of structured participant and non-participant studies. We are not suggesting that observational studies are less valid than other techniques, but the primary interest we found in the field at this time was in studies using statistical and quantitative techniques.

The methodological caveats outlined earlier apply to interviews, surveys and records. However, each method has advantages and disadvantages. Interviews can provide extensive, in-depth information, but are time-consuming and require skill in doing the interviews and summarizing the results. Surveys can be administered quickly, are confidential, and can be easily repeated at different times or with other samples. In doing surveys, help may be needed with sampling design and questionnaire development, but once this is done, the package can be used in the future. The major problem with using records is that it is extremely difficult to use old records to meet current evaluation needs. That is, *records systems must be designed along with the evaluation* (more on records in the section on information systems). All of these data collection methods can be used to study program implementation and to evaluate program process and outcome as the remainder of this chapter will show. Whatever methods are chosen, *the study must be pre-tested* by trying out the instruments and methods on a small sample.

### Three Important Methodological Issues

In our review of previous studies and from our experiences in EAP evaluation we have found three major weaknesses (1) the type of criteria used to evaluate the EAP, (2) sampling problems, and (3) data analysis. Each of these will be discussed in the following sections. More information on research methods is included in the Appendix.

*Choosing the criteria.* How can we tell if the goals of the EAP are being met? In order to evaluate how an EAP operates and the impact it has on an organization, it is important to carefully plan the type of criteria that will be used.

The first problem that evaluators face in choosing criteria is that *reliable and valid measures must be used*. *Validity* essentially means that the instrument actually measures what it is intended to measure. *Reliability* means that there is little room for measurement error (see Appendix One).

The second problem of criteria choice is to find out what data are actually available. *Availability, or accessibility, is a primary problem when the evaluation to be undertaken is a retrospective one.* For example, when evaluators set up a study to compare current work performance with work performance prior to EAP intervention, they may be hindered by three obstacles: (1) the data may simply not have been gathered at that time, (2) the data may be protected by confidentiality standards, and (3) the types of data needed may have been collected by several different departments (e.g., sick days by the medical unit; number of grievances by the union; amount of benefits used by the insurance company) making retrieval cumbersome or impossible.

The third problem of criteria choice is to recognize that *the same criteria may not be appropriate for all employees.* (This is actually a type of validity problem.) For example, commonly used records of tardiness, absenteeism, accidents, etc. may not be kept on white collar employees, and/or may not accurately reflect their level of work performance. Because white collar employees' work is often less tangible than that of blue collar workers', the evaluator may have to use more creativity in choosing criteria to measure work performance of white-collar and senior level managers.

*A fourth problem to be aware of in choosing criteria is that of comparability.* It is useful to use criteria that are comparable to those used in other evaluation studies. For example, if one evaluation study chooses rates of absenteeism to reflect a level of work performance and another chooses supervisor's ratings, we cannot easily compare the results of these two evaluations.

*Choosing the sample.* Initially it may appear to be quite obvious that the sample to study when evaluating an EAP is the group of employees who use the EAP. In fact, this is the sample that most evaluation studies to date have described. However, as Figure 2 illustrates, *choosing this sample may provide us with rather limited data and biased results.* It may be important to describe the number, characteristics, and outcome of employees who refuse their supervisors' referral to the EAP (Box #3), who refuse to accept the recommendations by the EAP counselors (Box #8), or who leave the organization after using the EAP (Box #10). Simply describing the "cooperative" employees who come in contact with the EAP may inflate the EAP's success rate.

A second consideration in choosing a sample is *the need for a comparison group*. For example, let us imagine an evaluation that reports, "75% of employees who used the EAP improved on work performance criteria x, y, and z." Improved compared to what? One option is to compare their work performance level after using the EAP to their work performance level prior to intervention. Essentially this is using themselves as their own comparison group. However, this method raises two problems: (1) The employees may have changed simply because of *maturation*, not because of the EAP intervention. Therefore, it is important that the sample be studied for long enough periods of time. This may particularly occur with samples of young employees who improve with age or with samples of employees, early in their careers, who improve with job experience; (2) secondly, the sample may show change largely because of *extraneous factors,* e.g., increased benefits, salary increases, lay-offs, strikes, etc. which may affect the work performance criteria of *all* employees.

A second, or better, option is to choose a comparison group comprised of other employees. Depending on the goals of the evaluation, appropriate comparison groups may be (1) employees of the organization not using the EAP, or (2) employees who are identified as having problems, but do not use the EAP (Boxes #3 and/or #8 in Figure 1). Perhaps an ideal comparison group would be troubled employees who receive no help at all (Box #6). However, obtaining this sample would require screening of the entire employee population in order to detect the troubled employees who are neither referred to the EAP nor seek help on their own.

The type of sample chosen by an evaluator may depend on the limits of the study and the availability of data on employees. Some evaluations are intended to be rather small scale, and in this case, the evaluator may want to simply describe changes within a sample before and after intervention. However, even in the most limited evaluation, it is important to be able to describe (1) how the sample was chosen, (2) how the sample compares to the general population (i.e. all employees) in terms of basic demographics (See Figure 3), and (3) what limitations the sample selection may present in summarizing the results.

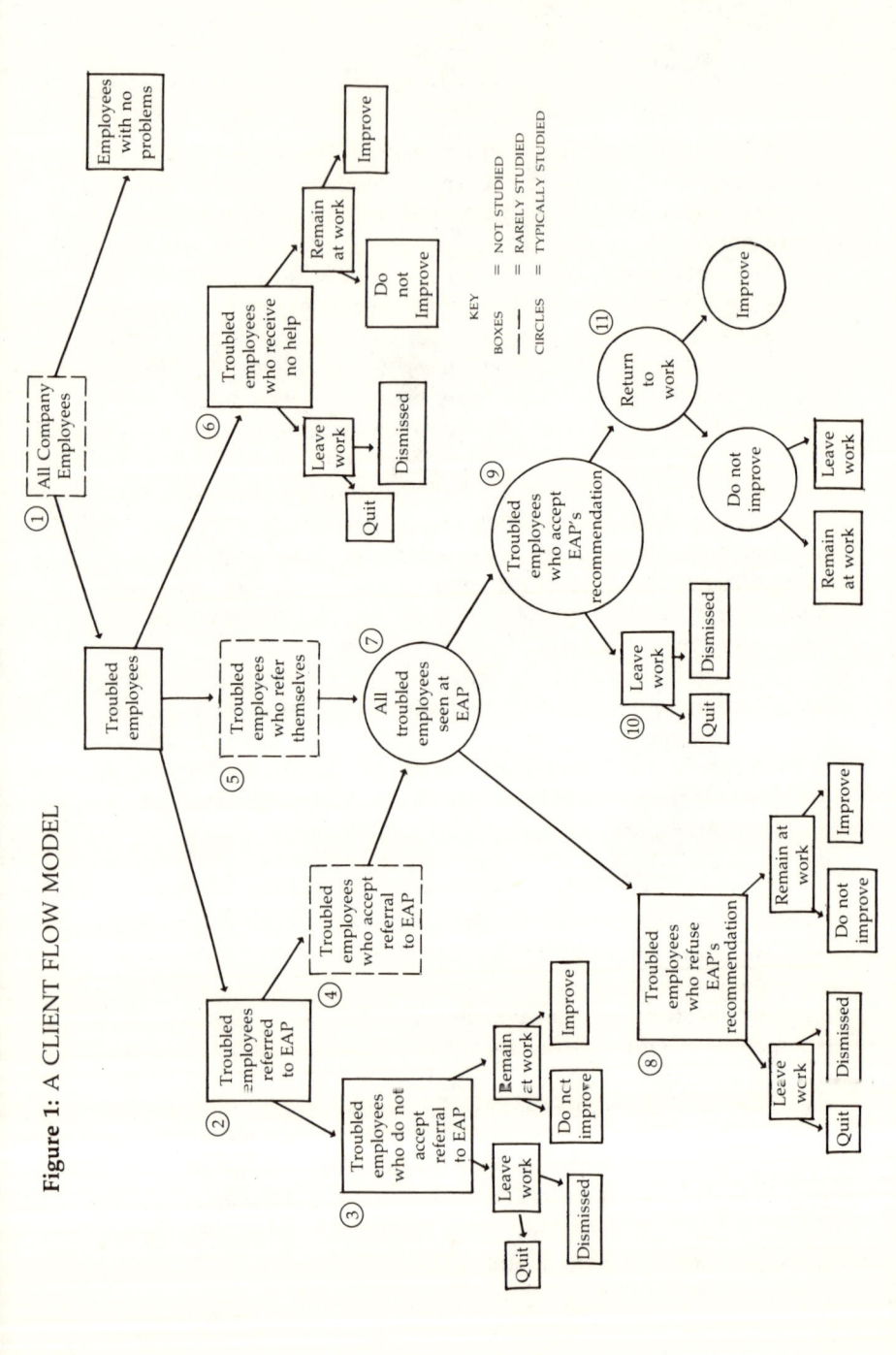

Figure 1: A CLIENT FLOW MODEL

*Analyzing the data.* Once an evaluation has been planned in regard to appropriate criteria and samples, it is important to plan exactly how the data will be analyzed. First, it is important to either understand basic statistics or consult with people knowledgeable in this area. While we will not describe methods of statistical analyses in this review, it is important to note that *the types of analyses appropriate for use depend on the size and representativeness of the sample.* In very small samples or samples that are not representative of the larger population, citing results that are "statistically significant" is misleading.

Another problem is defining and choosing the methods of combining data into "formulas." For example, many evaluations report on penetration rate, (i.e., the "measure of the extent which the program is reaching its target population," [Schlenger and Hayward, 1976]). This rate is most often used by alcohol-only program evaluators, to reflect the proportion of problem drinkers in the organization that have been identified and referred to treatment. Schlenger and Hayward (1976) in a well-thought-out analysis of the problems involved in computing a penetration rate, suggest the formula shown in Figure 2.

*Programs differ in the type of penetration rate they use.* They may estimate the proportion of problem drinkers in the work force (part of the denominator) which may vary from 3% to 10%, but they may not take important variables into consideration such as employee turnover and/or recovery rates of those referred for treatment. Or, the evaluator may simply neglect to report what variables (and formula) she or he is using to compute the penetration rate.

A compounding problem is that, although the penetration rate formula suggested by Schlenger and Hayward is a good one for alcohol-only programs, *there is no accepted formula for computing penetration rates of broadbrush programs.* Estimates of prevalence rates of all assorted problems (e.g., marital, alcohol, psychological, financial, etc.) are likely to be widely fluctuating and generally inaccurate, resulting in penetration rates that would reflect formula inconsistencies rather than program differences.

Another formula sometimes reported in evaluation reports is that of *utilization rate,* (i.e., what proportion of the eligible population has used EAP services). Utilization rate equals the number of cases treated by the EAP divided by the number of eligible cases. This rate is different from the penetration rate in that it implies *no* assumptions about prevalence rates of those in need of services or number of clients who recover. If 25 employees out of a total of 100 eligible employees of organization X receive services from the EAP during the study period, the utilization rate equals 25%. There are two possible problems that may affect the computation of utilization rate (1) what constitutes a "case," and (2) what is considered "service" by an EAP? In simple situations, a case equals one employee. However, in EAPs where employees' dependents are eligible, it may be better to consider a case as one family. In simple situations, a unit of service may constitute at least one session with an EAP counselor. Some EAPs may define a unit of service differently (e.g., one telephone contact), which needs to be clearly defined in the evaluation report.

In summary, two points are most important to consider when preparing to analyze data from evaluation studies (1) use statistics and formulas that are appropriate for the data, and (2) include in the report an explanation and rationale for the analysis used. Reports on the utilization of Hazelden's Employee Assistance Services list number of employees using the program and number of cases (employees and family jointly assessed). A family member seeking help for him- or herself only is one case. Data are reported quarterly, and year-to-date. Cases and employee counts are not carried over into the next year. The utilization rate is calculated by dividing cases by eligible employees. We are avoiding the term "penetration rate" until such time as we have a better measure of the extent of troubled employees in the workplace. In the future we expect data on units of service to be more useful for program management than simply the number of users (e.g., hours of direct counseling time). For a good discussion of penetration rates see Hunt and Trice, 1981.

With these methodological suggestions in mind, we can now turn to evaluation techniques. Table 3 displays the various methods that can be used (column 4) and what questions will be

## Figure 2:
### PENETRATION RATE FORMULA AND EXAMPLE

Penetration rates given the following assumptions: 3000 employees, 10% annual turnover, 6% prevalence rate, and a constant rate of 36 referrals per year, of which 27 are successfully treated and retain their jobs.

| Year | Method | |
|---|---|---|
| 1 | $PR = \dfrac{36}{(.06)(3000+300)}$ | $= 18.2\%$ |
| 2 | $PR = \dfrac{36}{(.06)(3000+300)-27}$ | $= 21.1\%$ |
| 3 | $PR = \dfrac{36}{(.06)(3000+300)-54}$ | $= 25.0\%$ |
| 4 | $PR = \dfrac{36}{(.06)(3000+300)-81}$ | $= 30.8\%$ |
| 5 | $PR = \dfrac{36}{(.06)(3000+300)-108}$ | $= 40.0\%$ |

$$PR = \text{Penetration Rate} = \dfrac{PD}{(A)(E+H)-C}$$

where:
- $PD_1$ = Number of problem drinkers identified and referred to treatment during the time period
- $A$ = The estimated proportion of problem drinkers in the work force
- $E$ = Number of employees at the beginning of the time period
- $H$ = Number of employees hired during the time period
- $C$ = Number of people who are successfully treated and retain their jobs

(From Schlenger & Hayward, 1976)

answered (column 3) by that method. The last two columns in the table indicate the level of difficulty and resources needed. We will approach each type of evaluation as a needs assessment, process, or impact study (column 2).

## Table 3
## GOALS AND METHODS OF EVALUATION

| Purpose | Evaluation Type | Questions Asked | Method | Type of Information | Research Expertise Needed | Time and Resources |
|---|---|---|---|---|---|---|
| To determine the need for an EAP | Needs Assessment | How many troubled employees are in our company? What types of problems do our employees have? | 1. Surveys | Self-report of employees attitudes and needs | High | Medium |
| | | | 2. Interviews | Structured interview data | High | High |
| | | How many employees would use an EAP? What barriers are there to EAP implementation? | 3. Key informant studies | Responses from key persons in the company | Low | Low |
| | | | 4. Archival studies | Data in employee records | Medium | Medium |
| | | What are the best treatment resources available to us for client referral? | Survey of referral sources | —Interviews/questions from/to local (or other) treatment facilities | Low | Low |
| To measure the activities and efficiency of the EAP; degree of program implementation | Process Evaluation | Who is using the EAP? (utilization and penetration rate) Was the program implemented as planned? | 1. Records | Count of number of referrals to EAP; count of number of employees refusing referral; comparison of utilization rates among company population of men/women; long/short tenure; white/blue collar, etc. | | Low |
| | | What proportion of troubled employees are using the EAP? | 2. Management Information System | Records of number of employees who refuse and accept supervisor's referrals | Low | Low |
| | | How effective is our employee orientation about the EAP? Are our supervisors adequately trained to make referrals? Are supervisory referrals effective? | 1. Training evaluations | Employee surveys; training evaluations Pre-post testing of supervisors after training; examination of referral rates by supervisors | Medium | Medium |
| | | | 2. Records/Information systems | | Low | Low |
| | | Is the EAP decreasing or helping to resolve grievances? Is the EAP saving the company money? | Analysis of job performance records | —reliable records of absenteeism —objective ratings of work performance by supervisor | | |

| | | | | | |
|---|---|---|---|---|---|
| To demonstrate the impact and effects of the EAP | Impact Evaluation | Is there a reduction in the employee's:<br>—absenteeism<br>—job performance problems? | —record of number and type of grievances filed<br>—records of absenteeism, tardiness<br>—records of alcohol-related accidents<br>—records of sickness and disability benefits, worker's compensation, insurance, etc.<br>—records of cost of EAP itself | High | High |
| | | Are troubled employees being helped? e.g., are there improvements in:<br>—maintaining/improving their job status?<br>—drinking decrease/abstinence?<br>—quality of life?<br>—resolution of non-alcohol-related problems* | Client follow-up studies | High | High |
| | | Why do some refuse referral? After referral and treatment, do employees have any problems in reintegration at work? What is the employee/client's perception of improvement and program effectiveness? Are the employees satisfied with the EAP? What changes would they perceive as helpful? (e.g., do the clients perceive EAP recommendations as appropriate; were they treated with courtesy; was confidentiality respected, etc.) Are supervisors satisfied with the EAP? (e.g. is the EAP readily available to them; have referrals been handled well, etc.) | Employee survey<br><br>Self-reports from employees | Medium | Low |

*Adapted from Attkisson, et al. (1978:228).

## NEEDS ASSESSMENT STUDIES

The purpose of a needs assessment study is to determine the need for an employee assistance program and to collect information that can help define the program model, the information and communication needs of the employee, and to aid in the implementation of the employee assistance program. In doing needs assessment there are at least three basic approaches that can be used. *Surveys* of all employees, or perhaps a certain group of employees such as supervisors, can be given to ask about the kinds of concerns they would have about the employee assistance program, the types of problems they may need help with, and any barriers that they might foresee in using an employee assistance program. Table 4 lists items that could be used in a questionnaire mailed to employees and Table 5 shows results from a study conducted by the authors. Also, by surveying or interviewing employees before implementation, awareness and interest in the employee assistance program will be raised.

Another alternative would be to take a smaller sample of persons and *interview* them, particularly a representative group of employees, supervisors, union representatives, etc. Interviews collect more in-depth information concerning the need for the employee assistance program. Another option that can be used alone or in combination with either surveys or interviews would be to use some variation of a *key informant approach* (Attkisson, 1978). By using a structured group process, key people who are important to the employee assistance program can be brought together to develop the model, implementation plan and standards for success.

Finally, the last approach would be to *analyze records* on job performance, accidents, etc., to demonstrate the need for an EAP. However, the data or access to confidential files may not be available.

Many employee assistance programs have been developed without any collection of data before the program is started. As a result there have been tremendous problems in implementation and employee acceptance. By doing a needs assessment, the program can be better designed. The data collected before a program is implemented can be compared with data collected after the EAP has been operating to measure the program's impact. Once the need for a program has been documented, the next evaluation issue is to assess whether the implementation and utilization of the EAP is consistent with company expectations. These are issues we will consider under the next section on process evaluation.

## PROCESS EVALUATION

Process evaluation is primarily concerned with what the program is doing. As shown in Table 3, there are a number of questions that can be answered through a process study with different methods for monitoring the activities and implementation of an employee assistance program. Process evaluation would study such areas as counselor activity, referral rates, utilization of the EAP, and effectiveness of training and written materials. Almost every single employee assistance program that we surveyed or interviewed collected some type of process data. This consisted primarily of reports to senior management on the number of employees seen and the activities of the employee assistance program staff. However, in almost all of these cases there was not any systematic way of collecting and analyzing information on the program.

### Studies of Program Implementation

In this section we will review three studies beginning with an opinion survey of executives of the Fortune 500 organizations conducted by Opinion Research Corporation for NIAAA in 1979. Earlier surveys for comparison were conducted in 1972, 1974, and 1976. The surveys reported on executives' knowledge and beliefs about alcohol problems and EAPs in their organizations. The second study was a survey done by the Washington Business Group on Health (WBGH) on employee assistance programs in 68 organizations. The third study, done by Trice et al., (1978), was a survey of supervisors, directors of units, and alcoholism coordinators concerning their EAP policy. Involving over 600 management-level personnel, the study also included training in federal units employing civilians in Northeastern U.S.

The Fortune 500 survey reported on program support, rather

**Table 4**

POSSIBLE AREAS ON A NEEDS ASSESSMENT QUESTIONNAIRE

Extent of Employee Problems:
— family
— alcohol/drugs
— emotional/psychological
— job
— legal
— financial
— etc.

Effect of Problems on Job Performance
Perception of Need for an EAP
Possible Barriers to Using an EAP
For Supervisors:
— past experience with troubled employees
— attitudes towards an EAP
Respondent Data:
— demographic information (age, sex, etc.)
— employment variables (job, tenure, etc.)

**Table 5**

EXAMPLE — Frequency of Reported Employee Problems on a Needs Assessment Survey
($N=181$)

| Problems with: | Percentage of Respondents Who Said They: | |
|---|---|---|
| | Have This Problem | Do Not Have This Problem |
| Handling job-related stress | 35% | 65% |
| Relating to your husband/wife | 25% | 75% |
| Handling psychological/ emotional problems | 24% | 76% |
| Managing personal finances | 19% | 81% |
| Raising children | 19% | 81% |
| Dealing with alcohol or drug problems | 13% | 87% |
| Handling legal problems | 12% | 88% |

than initiation, which may be somewhat different. In this survey, 83% of the executives reported that their program is strongly supported by top management. This support appeared to be a large increase from 1972, when management support was reported to be only 51%. When asked about union support, 53% of the executives reported strong support from the union, compared to only 23% in 1976. Seventy-two percent of the executives with company EAPs said their organization has a written policy, and of those with an organization policy, 84% say they read it. This was improvement since 1976, when only 64% said that their organization had a written policy.

In the WBGH survey, 40% said that top management alone initiated the program, 24% said that the program was initiated by both management and the medical department, 20% said the medical department alone initiated the program, and 11% said labor and management together initiated the program.

In the study of federal civilian programs, Trice et al. found that the presence of a union in the organization correlated with increased use of the alcohol-treatment policy. Over a three year period, 13% of supervisors in units with a union present used the policy, but only 6% of supervisors in non-union units used the policy. They found this trend to be especially noticeable in supervisors of unskilled employees. (For a balanced discussion of union-management cooperation, see Trice, Hunt, & Beyer, 1977.)

The federal government study done by Trice et al. reported that policy development may not always be as adequate as is usually assumed. They found that the alcohol program policy was not well-known. By the time the information traveled down the hierarchy from directors to supervisors, much of it was "trimmed" or converted to oral information. When the supervisors were asked to rate their familiarity with nine aspects of the policy, the mean rating was basically "unfamiliar." Familiarity with the policy was positively correlated with the number of forms used to disseminate information, training time, organizational emphasis, and the number of sources of diffusion. Because of these problems, there were disagreements between top management personnel and lower-level supervisors on some of the basic provisions of the policy.

The studies reviewed above are helpful in that they provide some unique information about factors involved in implementing an EAP. The main problems with most of the data from these studies is that they are based mainly on retrospective reports and may reflect opinion and selective memory rather than actuality.

It is puzzling that so few studies in this area have been done. It may be that evaluators in the past have been limited because EAPs lacked the necessary formalization (including written policies, training, and orientation). Another reason for the relative dearth of implementation studies could be because people may find implementation findings less interesting than client outcome studies. What is important to recognize is that *outcome studies may be inappropriate if implementation factors are unknown* or assumed.

The studies reviewed above do provide a good beginning, and from them we can recommend further areas of useful research and evaluation.

1. How does the source of program development/support influence program utilization?

2. How do methods of supervisor training affect rates of successful referral to an EAP?

3. How do methods of employee orientation affect rates of self-referral to an EAP?

4. Some researchers (e.g., Trice & Beyer, 1979) suggest that most current EAP policies are based on male employees even though the rate of female alcohol problems are increasing. How does sex bias in EAP policies affect referrals and utilization rates?

5. Will more employees use a broadbrush or alcohol EAP?

## Characteristics of Troubled Employees

Absenteeism appears to be the main problem characteristic of troubled employees. As shown in Table 17, studies indicate that absenteeism rates for problem drinkers range from 2–8 times higher than rates for normal employees. The study by Cole & Shupe (1970) reports higher absenteeism rates for psychoneurotics as well.

The other characteristics of troubled employees are less clear cut. Some reviewers (e.g., Trice, 1980) point out that, contrary to common assumptions, alcoholics do not seem to have higher turnover rates than other employees. The study described in Table 17 by Schramm et al. (1978) does not bear this out. However, in considering the importance of job turnover, Schramm (1980) quotes the figures of average U.S. job tenure as 6.5 years for men and 4.3 years for women. Schramm suggests that employers, then, may be accustomed to dealing with job turnover. In general, this may be so, but turnover in the ranks of specialized workers or management level personnel may cause many problems for the employer. Therefore, in evaluating and reporting job turnover, it is important to consider different subgroups of employees.

Research at Hazelden has found that, although many employees may need help, the number using the program is significantly less. That is, we cannot assume that all troubled employees will seek help. Furthermore, there appears to be variation across employee groups as to what types of problems they have. Absenteeism is the most commonly reported occupational problem, but a small percentage of the troubled employees account for most absenteeism. Our information system reports and employee surveys have also found variation in employee problems by client background variables, such as age and sex.

Most of the above studies reporting characteristics of troubled employees share the common problems of lack of objectivity and/or specificity of criteria. The absenteeism rate is probably the most clear-cut criterion; however, this measure may not be sensitive enough to detect troubled employees, especially in programs where early intervention is a goal.

Evaluators attempting to describe characteristics of troubled employees would do well to consider the following:

1. Choose varied criteria. Inclusion of both gross measures (e.g., absenteeism, accidents, job status) as well as more subtle or potentially sensitive measures (e.g., regular supervisor ratings, self-reports, description of nonwork-related characteristics) may help to provide a more coherent picture of the troubled employee.

2. Use comparison groups. In order to detect characteristics that are unique to troubled workers and not descriptive of workers in general, it is important to gather data on non-troubled employees. Cole & Shupe (1970) and Schramm et al. (1978) did an admirable job of accumulating and reporting data on comparison groups.

**Records and Information Systems**

The records of the employee assistance program counselor provides the base for much of the process information. This includes data on program implementation and characteristics of troubled employees. All employee assistance programs should, at a minimum, have information that will provide background data on the employees (age, sex, employment history, etc.), information on when and how the employee contacted the program and how the employee was referred, information on services provided, referrals given, and outcome of the referral. If this type of information is available in a file, then it is a simple process of routinely collecting and analyzing this information and determining the utilization of the program, and more importantly, the utilization of the program among certain groups of employees. (See Table 6.)

For those programs that are at a more sophisticated stage of development, a *computerized information system* may be necessary. Before moving into a highly sophisticated information system, it should be determined whether this type of ongoing reporting is needed. The reporting requirements were minimal for many of the persons we talked with, and it may be a waste of resources to spend time and money reporting data that nobody uses. However, if an information system is required, then we recommend beginning with a simple system that collects key pieces of information from the records and stores these in a standardized, easily retrievable format. Figure 2 shows a sample of a standardized form used by Hazelden that provides the basic information needed. One area that is often missing from most information systems is any data on units of service provided. As mentioned earlier, there is tremendous confusion in the discussion of utilization and penetration rates. We have almost no information on the actual amount of hours or other units of services spent with employees in an employee assistance program. In the future, questions concerning amount of time spent in training, travel, and direct counseling, may become more significant than simply how many employees were seen this year. Anticipate the types of informational needs that the program requires and build these into the evaluation system. We do not recommend putting all possible variables into the computer on the chance that they may be needed. In our experience, this overloads the capabilities of staff to enter and retrieve the data, with the result that the computerized information becomes a "black hole" in space — everything goes in and nothing comes out. Be sure that the manual records contain extensive documentation, but design a computerized system to retrieve selected key variables quickly.

### Table 6
### EAP INFORMATION SYSTEM ITEMS

*Coding Data*
1. Agency/program code
2. Client/case number

*Contact Information*
1. Date
2. Time
3. Reason for contact
4. Referral/information source

*Client Background*
1. Name and address
2. Demographic variables — age, sex, marital status, education, race
3. Occupational variables — current position, company and division, job classification, tenure
4. Employee or family member

*Assessment/diagnosis*
1. Problems
2. Most significant problems

*Referral Information*

*Services Provided*
1. Number of contacts, hours of service
2. Type of services

# Hazelden

**ASSESSMENT/REFERRAL FORM**
HAZELDEN EMPLOYEE
ASSISTANCE SERVICES

(For Hazelden's use only)
1. Agency code:
2. Hazelden client no.

3. Date of first contact: (mo) (day) (year)
4. Type of first contact:
 ☐ (1) telephone ☐ (2) in person
5. Date of second contact: (mo) (day) (year)
6. Your agency's case number:

## CLIENT'S NAME AND ADDRESS (if available)

7. Name of client:

Address: (Street or P.O. Box number) | Work Phone #
(City) (State) (Zip code) | Home Phone # ( )

8. Health Insurance:

## CLIENT BACKGROUND

9. Is the client: (check one)
 ☐ (1) an employee
 ☐ (2) a spouse of an employee
 ☐ (3) a child of an employee
 ☐ (4) another relative of an employee
 ☐ (5) other - explain: _____
10. Age: ___
11. Marital Status:
 ☐ (1) married ☐ (4) widowed
 ☐ (2) single ☐ (5) other - explain:
 ☐ (3) divorced/separated
12. Sex: ☐ (1) male ☐ (2) female
13. Number of years of formal education: ___
14. Client's occupational code: ___

## EMPLOYMENT INFORMATION

If the client is an employee or if the client is a family member of an employee, **complete this section for the employee:**

15. Employer Company:
16. Division or Unit of Employee:
17. Company Location: (City) (State)
18. Employee's Job Classification:
 ☐ (1) supervisor ☐ (2) non-supervisor
19. Employee's occupational code: ___
20. Employment Status:
 ☐ (1) regular full-time ☐ (3) temporary full-time
 ☐ (2) regular part-time ☐ (4) temporary part-time
21. Number of years with this company: ___

## CONTACT INFORMATION

22. Primary referral source (check one)
 ☐ (1) supervisor ☐ (5) diagnostic/referral center
 ☐ (2) family member ☐ (6) self
 ☐ (3) other employee ☐ (7) other - explain:
 ☐ (4) HELP Line _____

23. Reason for contact: (check one)
 ☐ (1) information only ☐ (4) other - please explain:
 ☐ (2) problem assessment _____
 ☐ (3) management consultation

## ASSESSMENT/DIAGNOSIS

Counselor's Assessment of Client's Problems: (check "yes" for **all** that apply)

| | Yes (1) | No (2) |
|---|---|---|
| 24. Educational | | |
| 25. Occupational | | |
| 26. Emotional/mental health | | |
| 27. Financial | | |
| 28. Legal | | |
| 29. Client's alcohol/drug use | | |
| 30. Physical health | | |
| 31. Alcohol/drug use in family/significant other | | |
| 32. Marital/or other significant one-to-one relationships | | |
| 33. Other family relationships | | |
| 34. Other - explain: | | |

35. **Enter The Number Of The Most Significant Current Problem:** ___

Service Utilization:
In the preceeding year, has the client: (check "yes" for **all** that apply)

| | Yes (1) | No (2) |
|---|---|---|
| 36. Used any EAP before | | |
| 37. Participated in inpatient/hospital treatment | | |
| 38. Participated in outpatient counseling | | |
| 39. Participated in individual therapy | | |
| 40. Participated in family therapy | | |
| 41. Participated in group therapy | | |
| 42. Participated in self-help group therapy | | |
| 43. Other - explain: | | |

**REFERRALS MADE** The following referrals were made for this client: (check "yes" for **all** that apply)

| | Yes (1) | No (2) | If "Yes" specify: |
|---|---|---|---|
| 44. Inpatient/hospital treatment | | | |
| 45. Outpatient counseling | | | |
| 46. Individual therapy | | | |
| 47. Family therapy | | | |
| 48. Group therapy | | | |
| 49. Self-help group therapy | | | |
| 50. Further EAP Assessment | | | |
| 51. Other - explain | | | |

**Figure 3 — EXAMPLE OF MIS FORM**

## HOW TO EVALUATE EAPS

**Table 7**
EXAMPLE OF EAP UTILIZATION REPORT

|  | Quarter | Year-to-Date (%) | Eligible Employees |
|---|---|---|---|
| Number of cases | 105 | 215 | |
| Utilization Rate | 6.8% | 6.0% | |
| **Client Profile** | | | |
| Family Status | | | |
|   Employees | 88 | 179 | |
|   Dependents | 17 | 36 | |
|   Average Age | 36 yrs. | 37 yrs. | 40 yrs. |
| Sex | | | |
|   Male | 45 | 42% | 40% |
|   Female | 60 | 58% | 60% |
| Marital Status | | | |
|   Married | 70 | 63% | 55% |
|   Single | 13 | 9% | 10% |
|   Divorced/Separated | 18 | 23% | 30% |
|   Other | 4 | 5% | 5% |
| Job Classification | | | |
|   Supervisory | 19 | 24% | 20% |
|   Non-supervisory | 86 | 76% | 80% |
| Seniority | | | |
|   Less than 1 year | 34 | 32% | 35% |
|   1–5 years | 29 | 23% | 20% |
|   6–10 years | 18 | 12% | 10% |
|   11 years or more | 24 | 33% | 35% |
| Occupation | | | |
|   Higher executives, major professionals | 5 | 4% | 2% |
|   Business managers, lesser professionals | 24 | 22% | 20% |
|   Administrative personnel, semi-professionals | 26 | 22% | 23% |
|   Clerical and sales workers, technicians | 21 | 24% | 25% |
|   Skilled manual employees | 12 | 12% | 15% |
|   Machine operators and semi-skilled employees | 9 | 8% | 7% |
|   Unskilled employees | 8 | 8% | 8% |

**Table 7**
UTILIZATION REPORT — CONTINUED

|  | Quarter | Year-to-date |
|---|---|---|
| *Assessment/Referral* | | |
| Referral Source | | |
|   Self | 68 | 142 |
|   Supervisor | 10 | 21 |
|   Family | 11 | 25 |
|   Other Employee | 10 | 21 |
|   Other | 6 | 6 |
| *Problem Assessment* | | |
|   Educational | 3 | 5 |
|   Occupational | 18 | 31 |
|   Emotional/mental health | 59 | 100 |
|   Financial | 10 | 17 |
|   Legal | 15 | 26 |
|   Client's alcohol/drug use | 7 | 12 |
|   Physical health | 9 | 15 |
|   Alcohol/drug use in family/ | | |
|     Significant other | 16 | 27 |
|   Marital/other significant | | |
|     one-to-one relationships | 51 | 97 |
|   Other family relationships | 29 | 49 |
|   Other | 14 | 23 |
| Total Problems | 237 | 402 |
| *Referrals* | | |
|   Inpatient/hospital treatment | 10 | 22 |
|   Outpatient counseling | 47 | 92 |
|   Individual therapy | 7 | 15 |
|   Family therapy | 5 | 9 |
|   Group therapy | 8 | 17 |
|   Self-help group therapy | 9 | 19 |
|   Further EAP Assessment | 2 | 6 |
|   Other — explain | 6 | 9 |
| Total Referrals | 94 | 189 |

## Training Evaluation

Another type of process evaluation is the evaluation of training of supervisors and communication to employees about the EAP. These types of studies can be easily done at the end of training sessions and we have included examples used at Hazelden. Many of the items that are collected have to do not only with people's attitudes towards the training, but specific questions on knowledge gained as a result of the training process. These items can be repeated again in later studies to measure the degree of retention of information about the program. We will briefly review previous research and then discuss some suggested methods.

Supervisors can be a crucial link between EAP policy and actual EAP use. Few studies have been done to examine if and how supervisors are trained to identify and refer troubled employees. Most policies stipulate that a supervisor's role is not to diagnose problems, but to document lowered work performance, and on the basis of this, refer employees to the EAP.

In the WBGH survey, 77% of the respondents said that training of supervisors was part of the EAP. Fifty-five percent of the Fortune 500 respondents said that training or orientation sessions for supervisors were provided.

The study on federal programs by Trice et al. (1978) found that supervisors estimated a mean of 2.5 hours of training time per year. (There was much variability, however, the standard deviation equaling 11.6 hours.) As described above, training time was positively correlated with supervisors' familiarity with the EAP.

Some studies have been done to examine the effectiveness of various management techniques. Latham, Wexley, & Pursell (1975) involved sixty managers in worker performance training using three different methods. They found that managers who were shown videotapes of good and bad workers to evaluate and discuss made fewer errors than managers trained less formally. This study is important because in most EAP studies or surveys of supervisor training, no information is provided about what type of training was used. Even more importantly, we are not given any indication about how knowledgeable the supervisors become after training.

Even beyond the question of supervisor training is the question of how supervisors actually perform in natural situations. In one study of 39 EAP clients (Kurtz et al., 1980), 22 of the clients said that their supervisor's confrontation was informal, and that drinking (rather than just job performance) was discussed. Most of them said that their supervisor's referral was in reaction to a crisis and not just the result of gradual documentation of job performance. This study is important in that it provides us with information about clients' views of how an EAP policy is implemented.

The effectiveness of various methods of employee orientation has not been reported. In the survey of the Fortune 500 executives, 52% of the respondents said that education was provided for all employees about the organization's program (this was an increase from only 36% in 1976). Also, 38% of the executives said that in-house posters and publicity were used to encourage employees to use the program.

In most evaluation studies describing EAPs, it is simply assumed that employees are fully and accurately informed about their organization's EAP. However, Heyman (1976) found that one half of employees ($N$ unknown) referred to EAPs in her study did not know about the EAP until they were referred.

Training evaluations, information system reports, and employee surveys by Hazelden consultants have found that training is an important factor related to program utilization. Employees who are knowledgeable about the EAP and believe that the program will be effective, accessible, and confidential are most likely to use the EAP. Workshops may be most effective in providing specific information, as most employees report that they only briefly glance at written materials. Because training effectiveness can directly impact program utilization, we recommend that the effect of training be monitored by evaluating training sessions, asking about training on employee surveys, and by studying the effect of training or program utilization. Table 8 is an example of questions used in Hazelden studies of EAP training. Again, the Hazelden monograph *Performance Benchmarks for the Comprehensive Employee Assistance Program* is suggested for those interested in detailed data from Hazelden studies.

### Table 8
### SUGGESTED ATTITUDES AND KNOWLEDGE ITEMS FOR TRAINING EVALUATION*

1. Will the EAP provide professional, effective care to the employees who need it?
2. Will the EAP be accessible to employees when they want to use the program?
3. Will the company benefit from this program?
4. Can members of an employee's family use the program?
5. Do employees have to pay when they initially contact a representative of the Employee Assistance Program?
6. Can employees who have personal problems other than alcohol or drug problems use the Employee Assistance Program?
7. Will the employer be informed when employees contact the Employee Assistance Program?

For Supervisors:

8. Can you recognize employee job performance problems?
9. Can you document employee job performance problems?
10. Can you make contact with EAP services?

*Note: These questions can also be used on employee surveys.

## Evaluating External Resources

This section focuses on evaluation of resources external to an employee assistance program. EAP practitioners routinely refer to agencies and individual professionals for the purpose of providing specialized or longer term service to clients. The referral process is an essential part of any employee assistance program. Comprehensive assessment skills need to be accompanied by specific knowledge of responsive and effective resources.

One of the biggest gaps in evaluation that we found in the literature (Stone, 1980), and in our survey of employee assistance programs (see appendix) was evaluating the quality of referral resources. The perceived importance of this area reflects the importance of the EAP counselor's role of broker. An effective broker matches the needs and motivations of clients with the best-equipped resources. The resource becomes an extension of the employee assistance program and reflects on the quality of the program. Evaluating referral resources is a way of measuring the overall effectiveness of an EAP. Because they are a primary part of any employee assistance program, the resources utilized need to be evaluated on an ongoing basis. Referral resources need to be initially identified and measured for their suitability, and then monitored for quality and effectiveness. What is presented in this section are criteria and methods EAP practitioners can use to evaluate resources. Attention is also given to cost considerations and subcontracting relationships, and some information about evaluation and health maintenance organizations is provided.

Criteria

Just what is it that one needs to look for? What information tells of the value of the service provider? Generally, the purpose of evaluation here is to learn of the availability and quality of services that accommodate the needs of the EAP and its clients.

The following are variables that can be used as a checklist in determining the adequacy of a resource. The list is not exhaustive, although it does cover the areas we think are most important in terms of making a judgement. What is most important is to know what you are looking for and to ask the questions that best direct you.

### SUGGESTED QUESTIONS IN THE SELECTION OF AN ASSESSMENT AND REFERRAL RESOURCE

A. *Professional Capability*
 — What is the history of your agency?
 — What is the professional experience and training of your staff providing assessment and referral assistance to our employees?
 — What is your staff/client ratio?
 — What kind of client problems do you prefer to handle? Do you refer?
 — What kinds of licensing/certification standards have you met?

B. *Access*
 — Where are your locations?
 — What hours are your staff available to see our employees or family members?

— What is the length of time between a call for an appointment and the date scheduled?
   — What is your capability for emergency response?
C. *Service Delivery Process*
   — By how many staff (and for what purposes) will the client be interviewed?
   — Once the employee's problem is identified, how is it resolved? What choice is the client given in the resources provided?
   — What is your policy on confidentiality? How is confidentiality maintained?
   — How do you follow up with your clients?
   — How are your services reimbursed? What is your fee structure?
D. *Program Maintenance*
   — What training or community education experience do you have?
   — What do you do to promote your services?
   — How will initial and ongoing employee orientation to the EAP be conducted?
   — What other ongoing publicity will be provided?
   — What are your methods of program evaluation? What evaluation feedback will be provided to us and at what intervals?
E. *Knowledge of Work Environment*
   — What, in your opinion, are the principal benefits to the employer of an EAP?
   — Is the agency familiar, or is there a willingness to become familiar, with basic aspects of our work environment (e.g., major products or services, employee demographic information, unique characteristics of the work or industry, normal work flow).

The above criteria can apply to treatment programs, multiservice agencies, and/or individual practitioners. When a number of resources are available, rating systems can be applied to measure the value of various resources more objectively. Often, three or four criteria measures are viewed as most important and take priority over other measures. For instance, location, area of specialty, and eligibility for third party reimbursement may be the three most telling measures of resources suitability. Numerous resources can be compiled, rated, and cross referenced for convenience of choice and retrievability.

## Methods

All EAP practitioners evaluate referral resources at some level. From periodically accumulating objective information to more sophisticated and comprehensive measurement, some form of evaluation is required.

In order to meet the needs of clients most effectively with a well-coordinated assessment and referral process, it is advantageous to have resources on hand and knowledge of how to access services. A place to start is a community information and referral directory, found in most communities nationwide. Resource directories are often compiled by area human service groups (AA, United Way, National Council on Alcoholism). Occupational program consultants throughout the United States frequently possess knowledge of available community resources (Wrich, 1980, Appendix). In some locales, comparative market data on various services, most typically alcohol and drug treatment programs, is available for a service fee. In rural locations, area mental health centers often have existing services and knowledge of other community services available.

Professional colleagues are often the greatest assistance in developing resources. Professionals involved in EAP activities in the same community are frequently in need of similar resources and have experience with available services. Professional affiliations like the Association of Labor, Management, and Consultants on Alcoholism (ALMACA), The American Association of Industrial Social Workers and other national and regional groups can be utilized for specific resource needs. Also, professional organizations such as these may compile shared resource lists between their members. Much can be done in resource development from behind the desk and over the phone. However, on-site visits and direct contact with referral resources can provide the most thorough familiarity with available resources. Impressions are created by face-to-face visits, familiarization with the geographical setting, the atmosphere, and intuition. These impressions contribute to making confident and assured referrals.

Once familiarity with available resources is attained, methods to measure ongoing effectiveness and quality can be utilized.

There is probably no better way of measuring resource effectiveness than to ask the users, the clients themselves. In the end, an important question to consider is "Would I go there if *I* needed help?"

This can be done by routinely surveying clients sometime after the referral has been made (See Figure 4 — Hazelden 1-month follow-up questionnaire). Routinely obtaining information from the service providers themselves through standardized questions is another form of survey that can be used. Feedback from resources on appropriateness of referral and client outcomes can be helpful in better referrals to client needs.

Attaining and verifying information from various sources is a valuable practice in evaluating external service providers. Using more than one method of evaluation increases the reliability of the information and therefore, it's usefulness. The list of evaluation methods below summarizes the options available to an EAP practitioner.

— client follow-up survey
— mailed resource questionnaire/checklist
— on-site visits/interview
— purchase of comparative market data
— survey of reference/colleagues
— personal impressions

## Subcontracting

Subcontracting is a way of more clearly defining a relationship between the EAP and external service providers. The capacity of any EAP to provide a full range of counseling services to a diverse employee population is limited. A major advantage of EAPs is accessibility to service. The practice of subcontracting can expand the limits of an EAP and further enhance service accessibility. In terms of evaluation, when the referral relationship is clearly defined, evaluation criteria are established.

Subcontracting can range from informal agreements to more formalized written contracts. An EAP practitioner is informally subcontracting when he or she establishes a relationship with a referral resource and expectations are discussed. The referral proc-

# Hazelden

## 1—MONTH FOLLOW-UP INTERVIEW
### HAZELDEN EMPLOYEE ASSISTANCE SERVICES

| FOR HAZELDEN USE ONLY | |
|---|---|
| 1. Contract: | 2. Hazelden Client No. |

3. Date of Contact: ___/___/___
4. Type of Contact: ☐ (1) Telephone ☐ (2) In-Person

5. Client's Name: _____ Home Phone: _____ Work Phone: _____
6. Eligible Employee's Company: _____

.................................................................................................

**FOLLOW-UP CONTACT RECORD**

7. Did you contact the referral(s) given to you by your counselor?
   - ☐ (1) Yes-which one(s)?_____
   - ☐ (2) None were given-why? _____
   - ☐ (3) No-explain: _____

*If client is covered by an HMO (Health Maintenance Organization), complete this section. If not, proceed to question #11.*

8. Did the HMO agree with your counselor's assessment of your problem(s)?
   - ☐ (1) Yes
   - ☐ (2) No-explain: _____

9. Did the HMO agree with your counselor's recommendation for a referral?
   - ☐ (1) Yes
   - ☐ (2) No-explain: _____

   If not, what other referral was made? _____

10. Did the HMO pay for the services to which you were referred?
    - ☐ (1) Yes
    - ☐ (2) No-explain: _____

11. Are you still receiving services from the referral?  ☐ (1) Yes   ☐ (2) No
12. Are you satisfied with the **referral**?
    - ☐ (1) Yes
    - ☐ (2) No-explain: _____

13. Do you need additional help from the Employee Assistance Program?
    - ☐ (1) Yes-explain: _____
    - ☐ (2) No

14. Overall, how satisfied are you with the Employee Assistance Program?
    - ☐ (1) Very satisfied
    - ☐ (2) Satisfied
    - ☐ (3) Neither satisfied nor dissatisfied
    - ☐ (4) Dissatisfied
    - ☐ (5) Very dissatisfied-explain: _____

15. Do you have any other comments? _____

16. Have you changed your address or phone?   ☐ (1) Yes   ☐ (2) No
    New address: _____ New Telephone: _____

| Name of Agency: | |
|---|---|
| City or Town: | State: |
| Person completing form: | Date: |

EVA 918 (9-81) Copyright © Hazelden Foundation 1982. All rights reserved     WHITE: Hazelden EAS     YELLOW: File Copy

**Figure 4 — 1-MONTH FOLLOW-UP INTERVIEW**

ess is better coordinated when the EAP, the client, and the referral resource have similar expectations regarding services offered, responsiveness, program costs, etc. Informal arrangements are the norm in most EAPs.

To insure a coordinated referral process, expectations can be spelled out in the form of a contract. This process elicits the understanding and investment of the referral resource and can increase the trust and comfort of the clients.

More formalized subcontracting can take place between an employee assistance program in one community and an agency or individual in another community. It is not uncommon for employers to have multi-site work locations. The subcontracting process brings assessment and referral services to all employees. A formal subcontract with an individual or agency spells out specifically what clients will be covered for what services, and how services will be reimbursed. Subcontracting with affiliate service providers requires complete orientation to company policies, EAP practices and procedures, and record keeping requirements.

Subcontracting for assessment and referral services extends the benefits of an EAP to employers otherwise accessible only by phone. The affiliate service provider becomes an integral part of the program and it becomes more important to specify expectations in a written subcontract. When subcontracting with affiliate service providers in various communities, the level of activity is dependent on the number of employees in that community. To better identify with the local service provider, the affiliate is encouraged to attend trainings, meet with company personnel, and visit the work site. A fee for service, as opposed to a per employee/per year reimbursement method may also encourage affiliate participation. It is also sometimes possible to receive a "wholesale" fee for service because of an EAPs capacity to effect and anticipate utilization.

Monitoring the quality of the affiliate service provider is essential to maintain coordinated management throughout the EAP. The initial identification and subcontracting process is primary, and ongoing monitoring procedures are also important. Affiliate service providers can be monitored through an evaluation system for all EAP clients. For instance, if client demographics, problem identification, and referral resource data are routinely collected, monitoring of clients' records can be a quality assurance check. Followups to clients and referral resources, if part of the EAP evaluation, also become a sound quality assurance practice for monitoring affiliates. The autonomy and integrity of the affiliate is not jeopardized through standard evaluation practices, and the "big brother" relationship can be avoided.

HMOs

Health Maintenance Organizations or HMOs have been the subject of criticism and praise since their onset. As service providers of health care, HMOs are increasing the services they offer, particularly in the mental health and chemical dependency areas. This has been a source of controversy, as some EAP practitioners find the mental health services through HMOs inaccessible, unresponsive, and short sighted. Many of the criticisms may be largely unsubstantiated or anecdotal. Proponents of HMOs see their mental health services as cost-effective and in keeping with the benefits employee assistance programs offer.

Evaluation can play an important role in this controversy. It can assist in documenting the level of client satisfaction with services received under HMO health coverage. Although employee assistance programs can bring the services of the HMOs closer to the employees, the EAP practitioner's choice of referral resources is limited to those services for which HMOs authorize payment or for services clients choose to finance privately. The practice of comparing responsiveness, accessibility, and client satisfaction with outcome between HMO services and other referral resources can play an essential role in effecting change. One method is the specific inclusion of HMO-related questions on a follow-up survey (see appendix). The same methods used in evaluation of other resources can be applied to evaluating the effectiveness and quality of HMO services. If differences can be documented, the employer's choice of policies can have a powerful impact in upgrading the quality of health care that HMOs offer.

## IMPACT EVALUATION

What the program does and how well it functions are important evaluation questions, but the bottom line in the program is impact. Logically, the process activities should result in healthier, more productive employees. We should always ask, "Did the program have an impact?"

Impact or outcome evaluation focuses on the degree of change in employee behavior and job performance following implementation of the employee assistance program. Again we would caution that because such a small portion of the employees may be accounting for most of the job performance problems *the EAP may not show major organization* impact. However, an evaluation will demonstrate impact on those employees using the EAP. There has not been much research on the impact that the employee assistance program has on a troubled employee. Hazelden has done several studies of both clients referred to Hazelden by their employer as well as employees contacting the employee assistance programs. In our case we have most often preferred to go to the employee to collect the data because of the inaccessibility or poor reliability of employer records. However, if there are reliable and accessible job performance records, these can be used in demonstrating program impact. If information records are not available, a follow-up study can be done. This would inform the client of changes in an employee's behavior or provide a measurement of employee awareness of and satisfaction with the EAP. This may include specific questions for people who have used the program.

### Suggestions for Conducting Follow-up Studies

As the following sections indicate, client follow-up surveys can be effective in documenting changes in the employee/clients' behavior and job performance following contact with an EAP. Client satisfaction should also be a component of a follow-up study. In doing follow-up, documentation of the employee's behavior before and after contact with the EAP is needed. Tables 9, 12, 13, 14 show items that can be included on the questionnaire. Also, information on the client, such as demographic data, treatment history, problems, etc., should be recorded in order to compare the outcomes of different types of clients (see Tables 6, 10, and 11).

Problems typically encountered in follow-up evaluation include:

1. Poor response rates. It is important that the employee's confidentiality be protected and that the employees have confidence in the researchers. Written release forms, full explanation of the study, and personal contact with the employee before the study starts will help in reducing refusals. Our clients have responded well to this approach, and we stress that follow-up is part of our commitment to the client and not just "another study." To that end our follow-up questionnaires include areas where the client can request help. Finally, high response rates require telephoning in addition to mailing questionnaires. We have used telephone interviews with excellent success (90% response rate).

2. Short follow-up intervals. Measurement of the employee's behavior should encompass as long a time period as is feasible. The determining factors may be time and money. A one-year follow-up costs more and takes longer to complete than a three-month study. Be cautious in interpreting results if a study covers only a few months. Also, if clients are followed over several months, regular contact should be maintained. Another problem with short-term follow-up is that the client may still be in treatment when contacted, therefore, the date of completion of all services is the best time to start follow-up. We have used a one-month follow-up contact successfully as a means of monitoring program quality, referrals, and client satisfaction (a sample of this form is on page 44). This one month contact also serves to help us maintain contact with the clients.

3. Sampling problems. Many follow-up studies contact only employees who return to work, obviously the more successful people. A random and representative sample is needed to have confidence in the data. Even with a good sample there will be refusals and non-respondents, but missing data will be lower in a follow-up study than in other evaluation studies, such as employee surveys.

4. Accuracy of self-report. We would logically assume that some employees may underestimate or not remember questions on job performance. In a recent study we found that supervisors reported significantly more absenteeism for the employee than the employee reported. It is also common to find out that the client's perception of his or her problems changes after assessment. If self-report is used, we recommend that these data be confirmed by a supervisor, other persons, employee records, etc., whenever possible. In the next sections we will give examples and discuss the results of some of the client outcome studies done by Hazelden. For a guide to doing outcome evaluation, see Spicer (1980).

## Outcomes of Employer Referrals to Hazelden

This section describes the characteristics and outcomes of Hazelden patients who were referred to treatment by their employers. The sample consists of 516 employer-referred patients in treatment during the years 1974–1978. To better understand the significance of the findings about this group of patients, we used as

**Table 9**

SUGGESTED CLIENT OUTCOME ITEMS

*Changes in Life Adjustment*
1. Change in those problems which originally brought you to the Employee Assistance Program?
   \_\_\_\_\_(1) Improved  \_\_\_\_\_(2) Stayed the same  \_\_\_\_\_(3) Worsened
2. Relationship with spouse/significant other .........................
3. Relationship with other family members..........................
4. Self-image (the way you think about yourself) ....................
5. Ability to handle personal problems.............................
6. General physical health .......................................
7. Financial situation ............................................
8. Legal situation ...............................................
9. Overall quality of life .........................................
10. Alcohol/drug use ..............................................
11. Job performance...............................................
12. Satisfaction with services........................................
13. Job performance (See Table 14.).................................

a comparison group all other patients at Hazelden during the same period of time (7,288 patients). This report is divided into two sections: first, a general description of the background characteristics of these patients, and second, a report of the outcome of the patients one year after treatment.

As a group, the patients referred by their employers were different in several ways from other patients at Hazelden (see Table 10). More of the employer-referred patients were men who were in the middle-age range. They were more likely to be college educated white collar workers.

The employer-referred patients also tended to differ from other patients in drug and alcohol related characteristics (see Table 11). Although both groups primarily used alcohol before entering treatment, the employer-referred patients were less likely to have used other types of drugs. This may be because the general treatment population consisted of more women and younger people, and these groups typically had higher rates of other drug use.

Employer-referred patients were less likely to have had drug-related hospitalizations or A.A. experience before entering treatment. A prior Hazelden study comparing employer-referred patients and patients in general found that employer referrals had a shorter problem drinking history (6.8 years vs. 8.9 years; Spicer, Barnett, and Kliner, 1979). Taking these findings together, the data indicate that *employer-referred patients entered treatment earlier* in their course of problem drinking. *Patients who were referred by their employers were much more likely to complete treatment* than patients in general (91% vs. 76%, see Table 11).

At follow-up, one year after treatment, 36% of all employer-referred patients who completed treatment reported total abstinence, and 27% reported less use. Only 5% reported that they were continuing to use the same amount or more of alcohol or other drugs. We do not know the outcome of 32% of the employer-referred patients because they were not sent questionnaires (e.g., refusals, deceased) or did not return the follow-up questionnaire. These outcome rates were similar to outcome of patients in general at Hazelden (see Table 12). A little over half of the patients in both groups reported attending A.A. regularly.

In regard to job status at follow-up, more of the employer-referred patients returned to their original jobs or were promoted than other patients. Also, *more of the employer-referred patients reported working during the entire year.* Both employer-referred patients

**Table 10**

BIO-DEMOGRAPHIC BACKGROUND CHARACTERISTICS

| Characteristics | Employer-Referred Patients (N=516) | All other Patients (N=7288) |
|---|---|---|
| Sex | | |
| Male | 87% | 69% |
| Female | 23% | 31% |
| Between ages 26–55 | 79% | 65% |
| Marital Status: | | |
| Married | 56% | 52% |
| Single | 25% | 25% |
| Other | 19% | 23% |
| Occupation: | | |
| Upper white collar[1] | 49% | 28% |
| Lower white collar[2] | 19% | 11% |
| Blue collar[3] | 26% | 15% |
| Unemployed | 3% | 17% |
| Other[1] | 3% | 29% |
| Education: | | |
| High School | 42% | 48% |
| Beyond high school | 16% | 19% |
| College graduate | 42% | 33% |
| Income: | | |
| Less than $10,000 | 19% | 30% |
| $10,000–$19,999 | 37% | 26% |
| $20,000–$49,999 | 40% | 25% |
| $50,000 or more | 4% | 10% |

1 includes professionals, managers, owners, and technical workers
2 includes clerical, sales, and service workers
3 includes skilled and unskilled workers, and farmers
4 includes housewives, students, and disabled or retired workers

## Table 11
### TREATMENT-RELATED CHARACTERISTICS

| Characteristics | Employer-Referred Patients (N=516) | All other Patients (N=7,288) |
|---|---|---|
| Pre-treatment drug problems* | | |
| Alcohol | 96% | 93% |
| Sedatives | 14% | 23% |
| Marijuana | 8% | 13% |
| Percentage who: | | |
| Had Prior Treatment | 6% | 9% |
| Had Related Hospitalizations | 32% | 51% |
| Had Prior A.A. Experience | 36% | 51% |
| Had Related Arrests | 31% | 36% |
| Discharge Status: | | |
| Completed Treatment | 91% | 76% |
| Did Not Complete Treatment | 9% | 24% |

*Pre-treatment drug problems total more than 100% because some patients used more than one drug prior to treatment. Not all types of drug usage are shown in this list.

and all other patients reported general improvement in their job performance, relationships with co-workers, and relationships with supervisors. The rates of improvement for the employer-referred patients were slightly lower than those of patients in general. This may be a reflection, however, of the fact that more of the referred patients kept their jobs and worked more during the year. Therefore, more of the patients in the total population with occupational problems may have simply quit working or changed jobs. Patients referred by employers, as well as patients in general, tended to report high rates of improvement in areas of personal growth (see Table 12).

When asked what problems they encountered upon returning to work, the employees indicated that their supervisors and fellow workers had little understanding of alcoholism. For example, co-workers expected the former client to drink with them. An obvious

## Table 12
### TREATMENT OUTCOME CHARACTERISTICS
(One Year After Treatment)

|  | Employer-Referred Patients (N=516) | All Other Patients (N=7,2888) |
|---|---|---|
| *Alcohol & Drug Use at Follow-up* | | |
| No use since treatment | 36% | 30% |
| Not using as much | 27% | 29% |
| Using same or more | 5% | 9% |
| Unknown | 32% | 32% |
| *Job Status* (1974–1975 patients only) | | |
| Worked during entire year | 60% | 46% |
| Same or promoted | 70% | 60% |
| Improved relations with co-workers | 70% | 74% |
| Improved relations with supervisors | 55% | 63% |
| Improved job performance | 85% | 87% |
| *General Personal Growth* | | |
| Improved relationship with spouse | 85% | 80% |
| Improved self-image | 90% | 87% |
| Improved ability to handle problems | 91% | 88% |
| Improved ability to manage finances | 73% | 71% |
| Improved acceptance of abstinence | 90% | 87% |
| *A.A. Attendance* | | |
| Attending at least once a week | 53% | 56% |
| Does not attend | 29% | 28% |

need is for education and training for all employees about alcohol and other problems, not to train them in diagnosis, but to make them better able to communicate with the troubled employee seeking to return to a normal lifestyle.

The major findings about patients referred to treatment from their employer were: first, prior to treatment, employer-referred patients as a group had fewer alcohol-related hospitalizations and arrests and had less A.A. experience than other patients. This suggests that their entry to treatment may occur at an earlier point in their course of problem drinking. Second, 91% of employer-referred patients completed treatment successfully. This is much higher than the completion rate of other patients (76%). Third, at follow-up one year later, 63% of employer-referred patients reported abstinence or decreased alcohol and drug use. Also at follow-up, a majority of them reported improvement in job-related factors as well as general personal growth.

## Follow-Up Study of EAP Clients

In the spring of 1977 the Hazelden Foundation was contracted to provide an employee assistance program for 6,500 public service employees and their dependents. The following is a summary of the first follow-up study of these EAP clients.

Hazelden's EAP uses the broadbrush approach rather than the traditional occupational alcoholism program model. This approach means that an employee or family member who has any type of personal problem is eligible to use the EAP. Counselors make assessments and referrals for emotional, familial, occupational, financial, legal, and health-related concerns as well as for alcohol and drug problems. The broadbrush approach assumes that any significant personal problem, if unresolved, can eventually affect a person's job performance.

Hazelden's EAP is located off the job site in order to maintain client confidentiality and provide the following services: information on the service and how to use it; a 24-hour telephone crisis counseling; assessment of presenting problems and other areas of concern; referrals to appropriate community resources; short-term motivational counseling; and management consultation for the supervisor of a troubled employee.

A sample of 100 self-referral clients and 9 supervisor referrals were included in the study. At the time of the initial assessment session with the EAP counselor, the clients completed the Client Questionnaire, a self-report of reasons for contacting the EAP, measures of job performance, personal relationships and abilities. During the first session the counselor completed the Initial Client Data Form which collected information on client characteristics, employment history, referral source, presenting problems, diagnosed problems, and recommendations and referrals given to the client.

All clients were contacted by telephone for a follow-up interview four months after initial contact with the EAP. The purpose of the follow-up was to help clients evaluate their own progress, to allow clients to report their level of satisfaction with the EAP, and to provide other measures of program impact.

Initial and follow-up data were also collected from supervisors for supervisor-referred clients. Supervisors reported on the referred employee's job performance and the supervisor's satisfaction with the EAP.

The average age of the sample clients was 34 years of age; the age range was from 22 to 64 years of age. Sixty-three percent of the clients were women, and 46% of those who utilized the EAP were married. Seventy-four percent of the clients were college graduates.

The majority of referrals (51%) were self-initiated and 43% learned about the Employee Assistance Program through written information (posters, wallet cards, and mailings). An average of three problems per client were diagnosed by the EAP staff. Family relationships and emotional/mental health problems were the most common problems (23% each), followed by family chemical dependency (12%), occupational/educational problems (11%), financial problems (10%), client's chemical dependency (7%), physical health (6%), and legal problems (5%).

During the initial assessment, clients were asked to rate the quantity and quality of their job performance as well as the use of employee benefits. Most clients felt their job performance was good. The majority of benefits and incidents reported were arriving at work late, leaving work early, and the use of sick days. Seventy-five percent of the clients felt their jobs were in jeopardy at the time they contacted the EAP. Four months later EAP clients reported improved job performance, and the use of employee benefits was greatly reduced (Table 2). Only 6% of the clients felt their jobs were in jeopardy, and over 80% were satisfied with the services they received. Improvement also occurred in the original problems leading to contact with the EAP.

Due to the small sample of supervisor-referrals, firm conclusions cannot be drawn about this group. At the time of initial contact, the supervisor's rating of job performance was lower than the clients' self-ratings. Excessive absenteeism was the most common job performance problem. Four months later, many of the supervisor referrals were terminated or transferred. It is clear that supervisors were using the EAP as a last resort; in most cases it appeared to be too late to save the employee's job. However, the employees and supervisors did not believe that the EAP was used as a justification for terminating the employee, but that the EAP did help the client and made termination a more humane process.

(For the complete report on this study, please contact the authors through Hazelden.)

## Other Studies of Client Outcome

Table 18 presents studies in which outcome of clients using EAPs is described. The data for each study are presented individually, and in some detail, to provide the reader with the most accurate overview of EAP outcome studies. As can be seen, it is difficult to summarize the result of these studies because they lack comparability. The most general statement one could make is, "a large proportion of clients who use EAPs improve." One interesting point not shown in Table 18 bears special mention. Foote et al. (1978) included clients who refused help and found no difference in outcome between these employees and employees who accepted help. Heyman (1976), however, did not include employees who refused referral. Presumably, this was also the case in Mannello's (1979) railroad study. These studies highlight the point made earlier, that it is important to specify which employees are included in the sample and what their respective outcomes are. To be able to understand the results of an EAP client outcome study this information is necessary:

1. What type of company or organization was the sample drawn from?

2. What type of EAP was used? (e.g., broadbrush, alcohol only, in-house, contractual, etc.)

3. How was the sample selected? (e.g., all referrals, employees who refused referral/treatment, etc. Is there a comparison group?)

4. Who is in the sample? (e.g., description by sex, marital status, work status, age, etc.)

5. How does the sample under study compare with other organization's populations?

6. What type of treatment did the clients receive? (e.g., inpatient, outpatient, A.A., etc.)

7. How long was the follow-up period?

8. What were the outcome criteria? Were they self-report, or were other sources used? Was there any effort to establish the reliability and validity of these measures?

Most of the studies listed in Table 18 do not provide many of the above factors, making it difficult to interpret their results. An exception is the study done by Foote et al. (1978). In their monograph, the authors not only describe the factors shown in Table 18, but also make extensive comparisons with the organization's population. This enables us to evaluate not only how much the clients improve compared to their prior work performance, but also can compare their performance (before and after treatment) to workers in general.

One major problem not addressed by any of the studies above is that most provide outcome for problem drinkers only. There are no studies in the area of EAP research comparing outcomes of clients with various non alcohol-related problems. Again, the study by Foote et al. (1978), is somewhat of an exception. It provides separate outcomes for employees in the categories of alcohol problems and drug problems, and "other problems." It found little difference between clients in these three groups in terms of intervention outcome.

**Employee Surveys**

Annual employee surveys can be a cost-effective way of assessing program impact. Employees and management may prefer the anonymity of a general survey. Several areas of program impact can be studied (see Table 13) in a survey, including attitudes, awareness, satisfaction, and utilization. Special questions can be developed for employees who have used the EAP and for supervisors. The major difficulty in using surveys is that they measure overall, general impact and collect less specific information than do interviews or individual client follow-up. However, we recommend that periodic employee surveys be used to monitor program acceptance and impact over time. By collaborating and conducting mutual surveys, several employers may be able to establish norms and standards for the field.

**Client Satisfaction Studies**

Another measure of program impact is client satisfaction. While the established EAP policy may attempt to ensure helpful services, clients' perceptions of the EAP can determine how successful the EAP actually is. The biggest problem in the area of EAP client satisfaction studies is perhaps that there are not enough of them to provide information to adapt and improve services.

Kurtz and Googin (1980) interviewed 39 clients who had a minimum of 2 years exposure to EAP services provided by their organization, a large public utility. Fourteen of the 39 felt that the first contact with the EAP was negative. "Negative," in what way, however, was not explained. In spite of this, though, 32 of the 39 saw the program as helpful.

In the report of problem drinking railroad employees (Mannello, 1979), 85% of the clients attributed their success to the organization's treatment program. Ninety percent of the sample gave "high ratings" to the program factors of staff competence, willingness to help, respectful attitude, trustworthiness, and confidentaility.

Client satisfaction can be assessed as a part of client follow-up surveys or employee surveys. We have found that the employee's perception of confidentiality is important in predicting use of the EAP and recommend that confidentiality be an item on needs assessments and training evaluations. For example, in a recent employee survey the majority of persons who said they would *not* use the EAP thought their "boss would find out." In a questionnaire used to evaluate employee training sessions, we again found people saying that confidentiality was the reason they might not use the EAP. Interestingly, other attitudes that predict non-use of the EAP are that some individuals believe that "people should

Table 13

POSSIBLE QUESTIONS FOR AN EMPLOYEE SURVEY

Extent of Employee Problem:
 — family
 — alcohol/drugs
 — emotional/psychological
 — job
 — legal
 — financial
 — etc.
Effect of Problems on Job Performance
Knowledge and Awareness of the EAP
Attitudes About the EAP
For Persons Who Have Used the EAP:
 — satisfaction with service
 — impact and effectiveness of the EAP
Supervisors:
 — use of the EAP
 — impact of the EAP
Respondent Data:
 — demographic information (age, sex, etc.)
 — employment variables (job, tenure, etc.)

solve their own problems" or use the church and religion as support systems, and some employees report using private counseling.

## Cost-Benefit Studies: Findings

There have been numerous attempts to quantify the costs and benefits of rehabilitating troubled employees (See Table 20). In reviewing the literature, one generally finds one of three things: 1) the evaluator reports a dollar amount for costs and/or benefits but provides no formula or only a vague rationale describing how this figure was obtained; 2) the evaluator chooses a single percentage (e.g., 12%–25%) representing assumed decreases in productivity, attendance, etc., accrued by troubled employees; or 3) the evaluators derive complex original formulas to use in their report to summarize cost-benefit. All three of these approaches are illustrated in Table 20.

Generally speaking, it is almost always possible to show that EAPs save organizations money. However, some evaluators (e.g., Foote et al., 1978; Schwamm, 1978) have shown negative benefits (i.e., costs outweigh measured benefits) for some of the programs during the first year of operation. As these authors explain, this may occur because of large initial costs to set up an EAP and/or initial underutilization of a new EAP. This may also occur when the clients using the EAP are still functioning fairly well (i.e., early intervention clients) and do not accrue the usual costs to their organization prior to referral to EAP. Presumably, these clients would cost the organization increasingly larger amounts if their problems were not treated at an early stage.

There are many problems in doing cost-benefit analysis of EAPs, most of which cannot be easily overcome. As has already been alluded to, perhaps the biggest problem is lack of consistency in computation methods used by various evaluators.

A basic and crucial question facing the evaluator contemplating doing a cost-benefit analysis of an EAP is, "How important is it to demonstrate that EAPs save money?" The Opinion Research Survey of the Fortune 500 organizations found that saving money was *not* a major reason for developing EAPs, although a

## HOW TO EVALUATE EAPS    61

majority of executives believed EAPs did save their organization money. Curran and Klefhaber's (1980) survey of 68 major corporations found that less than half of the organizations with EAPs reported doing some sort of cost-benefit analysis. Evaluators interested in the theoretical issues involved in cost-benefit analysis are referred to the discussion article by Schramm (1980). His basic point is that most economic analysis of problems and rehabilitation are overly simplistic. Schramm recommends a "human capital model," the main basis of which is the fact that employers have differing proportions of investment in their employees, depending on the employees' work status and seniority. At this point, Schramm's model is more theoretical than practical, but serves as a much-needed reminder that currently used cost-benefit formulas may often distort or give a limited picture of actual EAP costs and benefits.

Doing a thorough cost-benefit analysis is probably out of the realm of most evaluators' expertise. However, for those hoping to measure economic aspects of their EAP program, the following are necessary:

1. Valid and reliable documentation of absenteeism both for the organization population in general and EAP clients before and after intervention. (Ideally, data are available for one year pre- and post-intervention.)

2. Valid and reliable documentation of all other work performance criteria (e.g., productivity, disability, accidents, disciplines, etc.) for the organization population and EAP clients during the study period (e.g., one year before and after intervention). It is important to choose criteria that can be quantified.

3. Accurate figures describing cost of the EAP program. Often, this cost is not included in cost-benefit analyses of EAPs.

Evaluators considering an EAP cost-benefit analysis should refer to the monograph by Foote et al. (1978: 59–87) for a discussion of the problems the authors encountered in choosing appropriate methods for cost-benefit analysis.

## Problems in Using Cost-Benefit Analysis With the Broadbrush Model

Listed below are other issues concerning cost-benefit analysis for employee assistance programs, particularly the broadbrush model.

1. First of all, it should be determined whether cost-benefit is in fact a major criterion for evaluating the success of the program. As Paul Roman (1980: 8) says, "Broader humanitarian goals are frequently the basis for management's financial support of a program." Cost savings may not be as important as they appear. For example, union support is often based on the effectiveness of the program in helping the employee and the satisfaction of the employees with the program, not on dollar savings.

2. The early intervention aspect of the broadbrush model means that many employees will contact the program *before* showing any significant job performance problems. The logical assumption is that the broadbrush model will show cost-benefit in the long run (Roman, 1980: 6). However, this would also require, then, a long-term longitudinal study to show that effect.

3. Many employee problems, such as declining job performance, are difficult to document and assign dollar values to. This is especially true for white collar and senior level management employees.

4. Not all troubled employees will necessarily show job impairment. Researchers (e.g., Schramm) have found that the alcoholic employee is often very good at hiding any job impairment problems.

5. Troubled employees are often a small minority of the employee population and may not impact general organizational indicators such as employee turnover.

6. We do not have standardized, reliable measures of job performance and agreed-upon ways of assigning dollar figures to these.

These problems associated with determining cost-benefit do not mean that cost-benefit research is impossible. But they do mean that, for the typical employee assistance program administrator and counselor, cost-benefit is a type of research that is probably beyond their abilities. Our research has found that there are many probable savings resulting from an employee assistance program. Table 14 shows the results of some research with one of Hazelden's employee assistance contracts. We found, as many other researchers have found, a tremendous change in absenteeism. As noted earlier, this change occurs primarily in a small proportion of those employees using the employee assistance services. In fact, less than 20% of the employees in this study accounted for 75% of the use of benefits.

However, the question of whether the program saves the employer money is a different question than whether the program pays for itself. In the early stages of development the program may not save much money, and there is no evidence that the employee assistance program will recover all of its costs. There is research

**Table 14**

COMPARISON OF EMPLOYEE JOB PERFORMANCE INDICATORS
BEFORE AND AFTER CONTACTING THE EAP

| Number of: | Use Before | Use After | Amount of Change |
|---|---|---|---|
| Times arrived late for work | 196 | 61 | −135 times |
| Times left work early | 120 | 43 | − 77 times |
| Times of other absenteeism | 56 | 0 | − 56 times |
| Times used Health Insurance Plan | 96 | 90 | − 6 times |
| Sick days | 158 | 126 | − 32 days |
| *Medical leave days | 41 | 75 | + 34 days |
| Accidents on the job | 2 | 2 | 0 accidents |
| Times Worker's Compensation used | 8 | 0 | − 8 times |
| Short-term disability | 0 | 0 | 0 days |

*Note: The increases for this item reflect the employees' use of treatment or health care during the four months after the initial contact with the EAP. One would expect the use of this benefit to decrease in the long-term.

supporting the cost-benefit of the broadbrush model, and we would suggest that, before conducting this type of research yourself, the evaluator refers to some of these other studies when discussing the cost-benefit of the program. Also, the evaluator can routinely collect (Table 15) cost information from the employees and if at all possible gain access to whatever records the employer might have concerning job performance, absenteeism, etc.

**Cost-Effectiveness Analysis: An Alternative to Cost-Benefit?**

Recently, cost-effectiveness analysis (see Thompson and Fortess, 1980) has been proposed as an alternative to cost-benefit studies. In cost-benefit studies the evaluator projects a dollar value for the benefit of an EAP compared to another alternative or other employee benefit. "Cost-benefit analysis is a practical way of assessing the desirability of a particular program or project and of comparing programs with one another. It is characterized . . . by a long view of costs and benefits." (Rufner, Rachal, and Cruze, 1976:3.)

A better option may be to assess how much it costs to obtain some outcome — cost-effectiveness. "Cost effectiveness analysis requires only that benefits be measured in physical terms." (Rufner, Rachal, and Cruze, 1976:3)

Cost-benefit is clearly much more complex than cost-effectiveness since cost-benefit requires a projection of future savings for various types of programs. For both approaches, it is necessary that program outcomes be quantified, most likely by dollars, and that all program costs be available. Figure 5 provides a breakdown of possible indicators. To present a simple example, if the EAP costs $100,000 and 20 employees return to work following EAP contact, it costs $5,000 to successfully intervene with the troubled employee. A cost-effectiveness study could also be used to show the ratio of dollars invested to decreases in absenteeism, without necessarily showing the actual monetary costs of absenteeism, which may be very difficult to determine. Cost-effectiveness evaluation can be used to compare alternative EAP strategies (a particularly important factor as resources become scarce) against a common outcome.

## Table 15
### SAMPLE JOB PERFORMANCE ITEMS

Using a scale of "excellent," "good," "fair," "poor," how would you rate your job performance in the following areas? (Choose one)

|  | (1) Excellent | (2) Good | (3) Fair | (4) Poor |
|---|---|---|---|---|
| 1. Quality of work............. | ___ | ___ | ___ | ___ |
| 2. Quantity of work............. | ___ | ___ | ___ | ___ |
| 3. Relationship with co-workers..... | ___ | ___ | ___ | ___ |
| 4. Relationship with supervisors..... | ___ | ___ | ___ | ___ |

In the last year, how many times have you experienced any of these events because of problems you or your family were having?

5. Used Health Insurance plan .......... ___ times
6. Arrived late for work................ ___ times ⎫ About how
7. Left work early ..................... ___ times ⎭ many hours of work did you usually miss each time ___ hr.(s)
8. Taken sick days..................... ___ days
9. Used medical leave ................. ___ days
10. Had an accident on the job .......... ___ times
11. Used short-term disability .......... ___ days
12. Used Worker's Compensation......... ___ days
13. Been absent from work for any other reason.................... ___ days
14. Filed a formal grievance ............. ___ times
15. Do you feel that your job is in jeopardy at this time?
    ___ (1) Yes — explain:_____

    ___ (2) No
16. In the last year has your job performance:
    ___ (1) improved   ___ (2) stayed the same ___ (3) gotten worse

**Figure 5**

PROCEDURES FOR MEASURING
SPECIFIC COMPONENTS OF COSTS OF ALCOHOL ABUSE*

| Cost Component | Information Required | Proposed Estimation Procedure |
|---|---|---|
| Absenteeism | Number of days absent by alcohol abusing employees, hourly wage rates of absentees, overall absenteeism rate of firm's employees | Obtain costs of absenteeism by alcohol abuser by multiplying hours absent by hourly wage rate; compare with overall absenteeism rates to obtain net results |
| Missed time at work station and other disruptions to production process | Hours of downtime and hourly wage rates of alcohol abusers and other affected employees | Multiply hours of downtime by appropriate hourly wage rates |
| Employer medical expense | Number and types of visits by alcohol abusing employees to employer medical facility; total operating budget of medical facility and total number of annual visits of employees | Obtain average cost per visit by dividing total budget of medical facility by total number of visits; multiply this average cost by number of visits by alcohol abusing employees |
| Accidents and injuries to others | Number and type of accidents; medical expenses associated with accidents and injuries; lost production time; wage rates of workers involved in accidents | Obtain direct costs of accidents and injuries by adding all direct expenses incurred by alcohol abusing employees; obtain indirect costs by multiplying hours of downtime by hourly wages |
| Damaged equipment | Replacement costs of damaged equipment; hours of downtime and hourly wage rates of affected employees | Obtain direct costs by assessing equipment replacement costs; obtain indirect costs by multiplying any hours of downtime by hourly wages |

| Early termination | Number of employees terminated because of alcohol abuse and number of replacement staff hired; costs of advertising for replacement; length and costs of special training program for replacement workers | Costs for specific individuals will probably not be available. Obtain average costs of replacing employee from the total cost figures provided and multiply by number of individuals who were replaced |

*From J. Valley Rachal, Research Triangle Institute.

# CONCLUSIONS

**What Do We Know About Broadbrush EAPs?**

Thus far in our writing, we have shown that there is little published evaluative literature on the broadbrush employee assistance program and that what has been made public often lacks research sophistication. However, from our interviews, readings, and studies done at Hazelden, we can offer these probable, if not conclusive, statements about EAPs:

- There are certainly many troubled employees in the work force, and this number exceeds the number using the program.
- Alcoholism in the workplace is clearly a major problem that is well-documented.
- The rate of troubled employees and the types of problems they have varies by employer and occupational group.
- The majority of employer costs due to troubled employees is probably incurred by a minority of all troubled employees.
- Employees with alcohol and drug problems will use a broadbrush EAP.
- Training and written materials can be effectively used to inform employees.
- Concern about confidentiality is a primary reason for *not* using an EAP.
- Employees' job performance and personal problems can improve following help from an EAP.

CONCLUSIONS 69

— The majority of employees believe that an employee assistance program is a valuable benefit and will support the EAP.

— Personal problems do impair job performance but often in ways not easily quantified, such as efficiency and concentration.

**Recommendations For Further Research**

In concluding this review of studies on EAPs, it is apparent many studies need improvement. Because the field of evaluation of EAPs is relatively young, studies thus far usually have understandable shortcomings. The better EAP evaluation studies have not been cross-validated, and in general, researchers have not built on each others' efforts.

Overall, our recommendations pertain to two main areas of EAP evaluation: unanswered questions and methodology.

*Unanswered questions:* Evaluations to date have concentrated on outcome studies of employees' work performance and cost-benefit studies. Throughout this review, evaluation needs in other areas have been alluded to.

They include the following:

1. What is the nature and extent of employee problems?

2. How does EAP policy implementation affect EAP utilization? What are the crucial factors involved in training supervisors and orientating employees? What are the minimal standards and requirements for an effective EAP?

3. What other objective criteria (besides work performance measures) could be used to measure client outcome?

4. Are the methods of detection and intervention currently used (based on male, blue collar, alcoholic employees) appropriate for all employees? (e.g., women, white collar workers, workers with non alcohol-related problems, etc.)

5. What happens to employees who refuse referral and/or treatment? Do some employees get better without EAP's help?

What factors are involved, and how could these factors be incorporated into employee's lives in general? (The question of spontaneous remission is addressed also by Edwards, 1975; and Saunders, Phil, and Kershaw, 1979.)

    6. What happens to employees after they return to work after treatment? The need for reintegration studies has also been pointed out by Googins and Kurtz (1981).

As more research is done in the above areas, further evaluation needs are likely to be discovered.

*Methodology:* The second area of recommendations, methodology, has also been discussed throughout the paper. To review the main methodological requirements, the following are important to consider:

    1. Recognize the needs, goals, and questions of those involved in the evaluation.

    2. Select criteria that are appropriate, accessible, reliable, and valid.

    3. Choose the sample on the basis of representativeness, not simply availability. It is important to at least account for the employees who refuse referral/treatment.

    4. Include a comparison group. It is important not only to know, "x% of our clients improve," but to know improved compared to *what*. Minimally, the comparison can be made to their work performance, etc., prior to treatment. In this sense, they are their own comparison group. Better evaluations, however, are done when characteristics of clients are compared with (a) characteristics of organization employees in general (e.g., see Foote et al., 1978), or (b) characteristics of a sample of employees who are not referred to EAP (e.g. see Schramm, et al., 1978), or (c) a matched sample of employees with similar problems who do *not* receive treatment.

    5. Use appropriate methods of data analysis and make clear in the evaluation report what formulas and statistics were used. If assumptions have been made, explain their rationale.

## Making Evaluation Usable

The employee assistance field is entering a new era of accountability. There is an increase in evaluation expertise among both employee assistance program staff and the research community. Throughout this paper we have tried to provide a variety of options for the administrator and counselor to use. We have also described the need for diversity in evaluation, emphasizing the areas of process and impact. In closing, we have some final comments and recommendations on ways that the utility of evaluation can be enhanced.

First of all, evaluation should be seen as a team project (Binner, in Feldman 1980:451), and other people should be involved in defining the purposes of the evaluation and assisting throughout the project. Evaluation is too often conducted in isolation from other staff. The result is that staff feels uninvolved and uninformed about the study, leaving the evaluator to guess what other people want to know about the program. Secondly, reasonable expectations about what the evaluation can do need to be set. Evaluation will not have an immediate impact, but will collect data that can be used for long-term planning and management. Evaluation is not the same as theoretical research. There are numerous constraints on doing applied research which should be discussed at the initial stages of development. As Attkisson (1978:61) says, "The question for an evaluator is not how much can be accomplished, but rather how much of what is accomplished is relevant."

The next point is that the evaluation study must be completed on time. If a decision is to be made in March and the evaluation report is delayed until June, the decision will have already been made without the evaluator's input. It is important to design studies that will be available when needed. In addition, we have noted a tendency in many evaluation studies to rely exclusively on written reports. In our experience, many people will only briefly glance through a report, and some may not read the report at all. Verbal reports, workshops, and meetings with management are important in communicating the results of a study. Both positive or negative findings need to be presented. There appears to be almost a dichotomy in the field; the evaluators spend most of their time pointing out the failings and problems with the employee assistance programs and the program managers pointing out only the strengths and benefits of the program. The reality is somewhere in between — the program has both positive and negative effects and the evaluator should discuss both, indicating areas of improvement and change where needed.

Finally, of course, the operation of the organization needs to be well understood. Again, evaluation must be designed to answer the questions of some key decision-makers. Use these people to help establish standards of success and expectations for the evaluation. We cannot emphasize too strongly the need for the evaluation to be designed with very clear objectives and clearly defined audiences in mind.

What can the program administrator or counselor do? He or she can keep usable records containing the type of information that can be used for periodic reports or store them in an ongoing computerized information system. Routinely evaluating training, and conducting periodic employee surveys are simple and cost-effective ways of providing evaluative data on the program. It would seem logical that more employee assistance programs should try to collect job impairment data both before and after employee contact with the program. There are, of course, areas where the individual employee assistance program administrator will not be able to conduct studies. Sophisticated client outcome and cost-benefit studies are probably beyond the means of most programs. Measuring the extent of employee problems in the work force may be a very difficult type of research for the individual program. Certain program models and staffing patterns make information-gathering difficult, preventing some types of evaluations.

However, there is in our experience a tremendous amount of expertise in the field that can be shared among the different programs. We encourage professional organizations at both national and regional levels to undertake the development of a training package for employee assistance program evaluation and also to establish conferences and consortiums for the sharing of expertise and methodology. We must avoid the continuation of each program doing individualized, non-comparable evaluation research. At this time, we need to make the commitment to move towards more standardized methods and criteria. From both our interviews and surveys of employee assistance program staff, our review of literature, and our research, we believe that employee assistance programs can benefit both the employee and the organization. But frankly, we were unable to demonstrate just how well these programs work. It is no longer sufficient for an employee assistance program to be available and appreciated; in the future, we must be able to validate what we do and what effects we have.

# REFERENCES

Attkisson, C., Hargreaves, W. A., Horowitz, M. J. and Sorenson, J. E.
1978 *Evaluation of Human Service Programs.* New York: Academic Press.
Borus, M. E.
1979 "Measuring the impact of employment-related social programs: A primer on the evaluation of employment and training, vocational education, vocational rehabilitation, and other job-oriented programs." Kalamazoo, Michigan: UpJohn.
Chopra, K. S., Preston, D. A., and Gerson, L. W.
1979 "The effort of constructive coercion on the rehabilitative process." *Journal of Occupational Medicine,* 21:749–752.
Cole, N. J. and Shupe, D. R.
1970 "A four-year follow-up of former psychiatric patients in industry." *Archives of General Psychiatry,* 22:2229–229.
Cronbach, Lee J. and Associates
1980 *Toward Reform of Program Evaluation.* San Francisco: Jossey-Bass, Inc.
Curran, G., and Kiefhaber, A.
1980 "Mental wellness programs in industry: A survey report." *Alcohol Health and Research World,* Fall:54–58.
Edwards, D. W.
1975 "The evaluation of troubled employee and occupational alcoholism programs." *Occupational Alcoholism Programs.* In R. Williams and G. Moffat (Eds.), Springfield, Ill.: Thomas.
Feldman, S., editor
1980 *The Administration of Mental Health Services.* Springfield, Illinois: Charles C. Thomas Company.
Foote, A., Erfurt, J. D., Strauch, P. A., and Guzzardo, T. L.
1978 "Cost-effectiveness of occupational employee assistance pro-

grams." Worker Health Program, Institute of Labor and Industrial Relations. University of Michigan-Wayne State University.

Foote, A., and Erfurt, J. D.
1981 "Evaluating an employee assistance program." *EAP Digest*, Sept. 10 ct:14–25.

Freedberg, E. J., and Johnston, W. E.
1980 "Outcome with alcoholics seeking treatment voluntarily or after confrontation by their employer." *Journal of Occupational Medicine*, 22:83–86.

Googins, B., and Kurtz, N. R.
1981 "Factors inhibiting supervisory referrals to occupational alcoholism intervention programs." *Journal of Studies on Alcohol*, 41:1196–1207.

Heyman, M. M.
1976 "Referral to alcoholism programs in industry." *Journal of Studies on Alcohol*, 37:900–907.

Hunt, R. and Trice, H. M.
1981 "Penetration rates in occupational programming: A caution about oversimplification." Working Paper #7.

Illinois Bell's Alcoholic Rehabilitation Program: Absenteeism cut, disability reduced, productivity improved. *EBPR Research Reports*. (author unknown).

Kurtz, N. R., Googins, B. and Williams, C.
1980 "Clients' views of an alcoholism program." *Labor-Management Alcoholism Journal*, 10:102–113.

Latham, G. P., Wexley, K. N., and Pursell, E. D.
1975 "Training managers to minimize rating errors in the observation of behavior." *Journal of Applied Psychology*, 60:550–555.

Mannello, T. A.
1979 "Problem drinking among railroad workers: Extent, impact and solutions." Monograph Series No. 4. Washington D. C.: University Research Corporation.

Marsh, M. S.
"Translating the model of industrial employee assistance programs to a university setting: The Campus Assistance Program at Washington University." Unpublished manuscript.

Milstead-O'Keefe, R. J.
1980 "Meeting the needs of working women with alcohol problems." *Labor-Management Alcoholism Journal*, 10:50–69.

O'Connor, J. A.
1975 "You're already paying for it — let's call it what it is." *Labor-Management Alcoholism Journal*, 5:11–16.

Opinion Research Corporation
  1979 "Executives knowledge, attitudes and behavior regarding alcoholism and alcohol abuse." A report of Executive Caravan Findings. Study IV. Prepared for NIAAA.
Patton, M. W.
  1978 *Utlization-Focused Evaluation*. Beverly Hills, California: Sage Press.
Patton, M. W.
  1980 *Qualitative Evaluation Methods*. Beverly Hills, California: Sage Press.
Phillips, D. A., and Older, H. J.
  1981 "Models of service delivery." *EAP Digest*, May/June: 12–15.
Plant, T. D.
  1981 "Education and prevention through employee assistance programs." *Labor-Management Alcoholism Journal*, March/April:166–177.
Presnall, L. F.
  1980 "A landmark employee alcoholism program." *Labor-Management Alcoholism Journal*, 9:165–174.
Roman, P. M.
  1980 "Employee alcoholism programs: Highlighting the 'goal problem' in evaluation research." Paper presented at the Evaluation Research Society, Washington, D.C., November 20, 1980.
Roman, P. M.
  1981 "Evaluation of employee alcoholism programs." *Labor-Management Alcoholism Journal*, 10(1):1–12.
Rufner, B. L., Rachal, J. V., and Cruze, A. M.
  1976 *Final Report — Management Effectiveness Measures for NIDA Treatment Programs: Volume 1, Cost-Benefit Analysis*. (FR234-1149) Research Triangle Park, North Carolina: Research Triangle Institute.
Saad, E. S. M.
  "Unemployment and sickness absenteeism in alcoholism." Reference unknown.
Schlenger, W. E., and Hayward, B. S.
  1976 "Occupational programming problems in research and evaluation." *Alcohol, Health and Research World*, Spring 1:18–22.
Schramm, C. J., Mandell, W. and Archer, J.
  1978 *Workers Who Drink*. Lexington, Mass: Lexington.
Schramm, C. J.
  1977 "Measuring the return on program costs: Evaluation of a multiemployer alcoholism treatment program." *American Journal of Public Health*, 67:50–51.

Schramm, C. J.
1980 "Evaluating industrial alcoholism programs." *Journal of Studies on Alcohol*, 41:702–713.

Spicer, J. W.
1980 *Outcome Evalution: How To Do It.* Center City, Minnesota: Hazelden Educational Materials.

Spicer, J. W., Barnett, P., and Kliner, D.
1979 The outcomes of employer referrals to treatment. Center City, Minnesota: Hazelden Educational Materials.

Stone, J. D.
1980 "Identifying, evaluating, and utilizing treatment sources." *Labor-Management Alcoholism Journal.* 10:114–125.

Study Evaluates Oldsmobile program. *Labor-Management Alcoholism Journal*, 4:35–38. (author unknown)

Task Force Report
1978 "Appropriate criteria for evaluating employee assistance programs." Companion Paper No. 2. Addiction Research Foundation: Toronto, Canada.

Thompson, M. S., and Fortess, E. F.
1980 "Cost-effectiveness analysis in health program evaluation." *Evaluation Review.* 4 (4):549–568.

Trice, H. M.
1980 "Job-based alcoholism and employee assistance programs." *Alcohol, Health, and Research World;* Spring:4–16.

Trice, H. M., Hunt, R. E., Beyer, J. M.
1977 "Alcoholism programs in unionized work settings: Problems and prospects in union-management cooperation." *Journal of Drug Issues;* 7:103–115.

Trice, H. M. and Beyer, J. M.
1979 "Women employees and job-based alcoholism programs." *Journal of Drug Issues*, Summer: 371–385.

Trice, H., Beyer, J. M., and Hunt, R. E.
1978 "Evaluating implementation of a job-based alcoholism policy." *Journal of Studies on Alcohol*, 39 (3):448–465v.

Two tales of one city (The Philadelphia Police and Fire Department Programs) *Labor-Management Alcoholism Journal*, 4:1–23 (author unknown).

U. S. Department of Health, Education, and Welfare.
EAP-intervention, review. Fourth Special Report to the U.S. Congress on Alcohol and Health.

# APPENDIX ONE
# AN OVERVIEW OF RESEARCH METHODS

# AN OVERVIEW OF RESEARCH METHODS

Good research design generally requires a high level of expertise. For a more thorough discussion on appropriate research methods, the reader is referred to Boros (1979). Edwards (1975) is also a good resource, providing insights on major EAP issues and methodological problems.

**Sampling**

As shown in Figure 2, one of the major problems in evaluation of employee assistance programs has been the lack of representative samples. Usually the persons studied are those employees who have agreed to contact the employee assistance program and who then follow up on the contact and remain at work. Groups that are missing from most studies of employee assistance programs are troubled employees who do not seek or get help, employees who do not follow through on the referral, and employees who resign or leave the work place. An evaluation report should clearly define the sample that was used in the sampling procedures. In doing research, there are a number of options in the area of sampling. First of all, a random sample of employees or of a certain population can be studied. This can be done by using a table of random numbers or some other method of randomly choosing employees. (If possible, this is often the best approach, particularly if you also have a randomly selected control group.) At times, a stratified sample concentrating on certain groups may be preferred. For example, supervisors may be given a questionnaire while employees in general are not studied. This procedure is acceptable as long as the report specifies how the sample was drawn and most importantly, whether there are any biases in the returns. Earlier in Chapter 2 we outlined some of the problems that occur from missing data and non-respondents. Again, all reports should define what group the returns represent and what groups are missing from the analysis (see Table 16). If there is accurate data on the employee population in general, such as age breakdown, sex, length of employment, etc., there are more sophisticated sampling techniques to measure the amount of error when using a certain size sample. Persons interested in this may turn to a number of basic statistical books that provide this information.

## Maintaining A High Response For Employee Surveys

If employee surveys are to be used as an evaluation tool, it is important to have a sufficient number of returns so that the data are representative of the original population. As noted before, the representativeness of the final sample is determined by comparing characteristics of the respondents with the original population. There are some specific steps that will raise the response rate, however, *it is very difficult to conduct a totally anonymous survey and assure a high response rate*. The number of returns will be increased to the extent that each employee is individually identified. Also, *survey costs increase as the methods needed to increase returns are used*. If it is important to contact all persons, we suggest a smaller sample and face-to-face or telephone interviews.

Listed below are ways to increase response rates:

1. Provide advance information about the study. Use the employee newsletter, notices on bulletin boards, or letters to individual employees prior to sending the questionnaires.

2. Personalize the introductory letters and envelopes; avoid pre-printed labels.

3. Assure the employee that the study is confidential in all communications about the survey; have the questionnaires mailed and analyzed by an external source.

4. Send a follow-up letter two weeks or so after the initial mailing asking employees to return the questionnaire if they have not yet done so.

5. If you choose to identify employees' returns (e.g., by numbering the questionnaires and indexing the numbers with employees' names and addresses) you will know who did not return the questionnaire. These people can be sent a follow-up letter, second questionnaire, or be contacted by phone.

Another technique occasionally used includes having a number on the questionnaire that is separated from the form and returned in a different envelope. Persons whose numbers are not returned would be sent a second questionnaire or telephoned. One enterprising surveyor had a drawing of returned numbers and awarded $50 to the employee with the winning number.

### Reliability and Validity

The data used in evaluation must be shown to be reliable, valid, and representative. Reliability refers to whether the information is consistent. For example, would different supervisors evaluate the job performance of the same employee in the same way, or would similar clients answer the same question on a survey in the same way are reliability questions. *There is no such thing as 100% reliability* — there will always be some error.

Validity asks if you are measuring what you're supposed to. We can all agree that baldness is not a valid measure of virility, but in evaluation studies, validity is a harder issue to determine. For example, does the job performance rating scale actually measure job performance? Reliability and validity are interrelated in that a measure must be reliable before it is valid.

Figure 6 illustrates examples of validity and reliability. In this example, assume that the evaluation goal is to determine whether having an EAP improves employees' physical health. Perhaps the assumption is based on the assertion that untreated alcoholics experience a disproportionate number of physical ailments and accidents. A valid and reliable measure (Cell #1) may be a comparison of sick days used plus number of accident reports plus results of physical examination the year before and after intervention. This is assuming that personnel keeps accurate records and that results of an annual physical exam are available to the evaluator. A reliable, but less valid, measure (Cell #3) is medical records data on number of visits to the medical unit by the employee before and after intervention. The department may keep reliable records but the data may not be valid because a medical visit is not necessarily synonymous with illness. An employee may visit a doctor to have his or her cholesterol level checked, to attend to a minor problem such as warts, corns, etc., or to ask for advice concerning an ill relative. Another validity problem is that a result of the EAP intervention may be that employees become more attentive to their health and, consequently, appropriately seek medical attention more frequently. Simply measuring number of medical visits may lead a researcher to believe that these people have become more sick, instead of more conscientious. Finally, an unreliable, and consequently less valid, measure is shown in Box #4. It is unreliable because an employee's answer may vary depending on how he or she is feeling the day of the interview and on how willing or perceptive they are in describing their health. There is much room for error, and the employee's response must be confirmed by other data.

Figure 6
CRITERIA TO ANSWER THE QUESTION,
"DID OUR EAP IMPROVE EMPLOYEES' HEALTH?"

|  | Reliable Criteria | Not Reliable Criteria |
|---|---|---|
| More Valid Criteria | 1. Personnel data on number of days ill, plus results from an annual physical exam before and after intervention. | 2. Not possible; a measure must be reliable before it can be valid |
| Less Valid Criteria | 3. Medical record data on number of visits per employee before and after intervention. | 4. Employees' answer to the question, "How is your health?" (good-fair-poor), before and after intervention. |

There are some established methods for studying reliability and validity. Reliability can be reviewed by having similar people use the same instrument in the same way, testing a group once and then again in a few days, or by repeating questions. Comparing these responses would give us the percentage of agreement — 75% to 90% agreement is common. Again, the lower the reliability, the more caution needed in interpreting the results.

Validity is harder to monitor, but some common approaches are to have "experts" review the instrument or to use different instruments (i.e., two job performance rating forms) and compare the results of the newer instrument with established standards from the other instrument. Caution is in order if the results are widely divergent from other studies; there may be measurement problems or the sample may be atypical.

The nature of the sample leads us to the last issue of representativeness. In evaluation research, particularly surveys and client follow-up, there will be missing data from non-respondents. If the people responding are different from the general population, the sample is biased and the results should not be generalized to all employees. For example, surveys tend to pick up people with a definite opinion — pro or con. Table 16 gives a hypothetical example. By reviewing this table (and using some statistical measures discussed later), we could surmise that younger males in labor positions who used the EAP were overrepresented in the study, and that the survey represented their opinions more than the views of employees in general. Finally, as we discussed earlier, it is acceptable to study a specific group, in which case the results in reference to that group only would be interpreted. Referring back to Figure 1 shows which groups we typically study and which groups we know very little about.

## Research Design

Two points to keep in mind when developing a research study are 1) the need for comparison groups, and 2) measures over long time periods. Repeatedly, we have found it difficult in our review of the literature to understand the true impact of the program because there is no data from any other comparable groups either within the program or from other studies. For example, we tend to concentrate on troubled employees who seek and receive help but know almost nothing about troubled employees who never seek help. Therefore, groups of people who have received different kinds of services or perhaps no services at all should be compared, if at all possible. The assumption is that more improvement would occur in people who have contacted the program than in people who had problems but did not receive any help for them.

Many studies suffer from not having long enough time periods to measure the impact of the program. During the early developmental stages of a program, short-term evaluation projects can be very useful in collecting the initial data on program performance. But as the employee assistance program matures, studies that compare employees' behavior for at least one year before and after contact with the employee assistance program are more useful. A hint in this area is to measure and control whether the employees are still receiving services. It may be that one year after contact with the EAP some employees are still receiving services and can-

Table 16

REPRESENTATIVENESS OF SURVEY RETURNS

|  | Characteristics of All Employees | Characteristics of Employees Returning a Questionnaire |
|---|---|---|
| Sex: | | |
| Male | 40% | 50% |
| Female | 60% | 50% |
| Age: | | |
| Mean | 32 years | 28 years |
| Median | 30 years | 27 years |
| % Who Have Used | | |
| The EAP | 5% | 15% |
| Occupation: | | |
| Managers | 10% | 5% |
| Clerical | 50% | 40% |
| Labor | 40% | 55% |

not be classified as having completed treatment. If at all possible, a better model is to contact the employees one year after completion of all assessment, referral, and treatment services.

It is preferable to have what is called a concurrent versus a retrospective design (Borus, 1979). A concurrent design studies the clients as they contact the program and move through the services. In this design the evaluation follows that group of clients rather than going back into the records and trying to contact a group of people some time after they have left. Concurrent designs are also preferable in that they have better measures of job performance and personal/emotional functioning before and after contact with the program.

It is important to be aware of different types of information. At the lowest level of information we have what are called nominal data. Nominal data are based on answers to either/or questions. Only certain limited kinds of statistics can be used with nominal level data. A higher level of data are called ordinal data, wherein a person provides information with some type of comparative progression. An example of ordinal data would be an employee who indicates how much improvement there has been in his or her job performance over time. Ordinal data are more sophisticated than nominal data and can be analyzed with more sophisticated statistical analysis. Most of us have a relatively simple time answering questions that are nominal or ordinal. That is, we can easily answer the question on our gender, and we have very little difficulty in saying whether our job performance has improved or not improved and to what degree over the last year. However, if we want to assign dollar values to job performance changes, then we have to collect more sophisticated data called interval ratio or continuous data. Total hours of absenteeism would be an example of continuous data. In this case, we can assume that two hours of absenteeism cost twice as much as one hour and that there is an absolute zero point of no absenteeism. But employees and supervisors may find it difficult, and even perhaps discomforting, to reveal this type of information. As we move up the level of data sophistication from simple nominal data to the ratio and interval data we often have to be more concerned about reliability problems, primarily because of problems in the ability of people to provide accurate self-report or the accuracy of existing record systems. In employee surveys, persons are more willing to respond to and more able to provide accurate responses for simpler items at the nominal or ordinal level. But in such areas as cost-benefit research, interval data is needed. We recommend that you not do what is so commonly done, and that is to say that "we *estimate* that the troubled employee is 25% less efficient, and we *estimate* that the cost to the employer is X dollars per day and therefore we *estimate* that the program is saving this much money."

**Data Analysis**

If the report will go to persons unfamiliar with statistics, these pages of highly sophisticated statistical analysis will confuse and irritate them. Present the type of statistic understandable to the reader and perhaps provide a second, more complex, report for those with a research orientation. There are two basic types of statistics, descriptive and inferential. Descriptive statistics do just what the title would imply — they describe the information. The use of tables and charts, percentages and frequencies, and averages are examples of descriptive statistics. When using descriptive statistics, the use of percentages with small numbers should be avoided. A group of a few employees should not be divided into many categories. It can be misleading when, for example, 10 employees are in one group and five employees are in another group and the difference is reported as 100%. When using small numbers, actual numbers must be reported rather than converting them into percentages.

Inferential statistics require more background in research and are designed to make inferences about the importance of the findings. They can be used to assess whether the differences between two groups are statistically significant or merely the result of chance; or whether two items are correlated at a statistically significant level. Because there are significant differences between two groups does not necessarily prove that the theory is correct. The differences may be significant only due to chance, or the wrong assumption can be made as to what is causing the differences.

Conversely, the fact that two variables are highly correlated may not necessarily mean that there is any causal relationship. Figure 7 presents a final point in the area of data analysis. In many cases the data will not be truly random or normally distributed. That is, the sample will be from an atypical group of people making it inappropriate to generalize to a larger population. This was the case taking job performance data from a sample of employees in the study conducted by Hazelden. Incidences of absenteeism were collected both before and after contact with the employee assistance program. We found that the information was highly skewed because a small number of employees accounted for almost all the absenteeism. This is not an uncommon finding in studies of employee assistance programs. However, it does mean that we should be cautious in using the types of statistical techniques which assume a normal distribution (i.e., parametric measures).

**Figure 7:**

NUMBER OF TIMES TARDY/PER EMPLOYEE

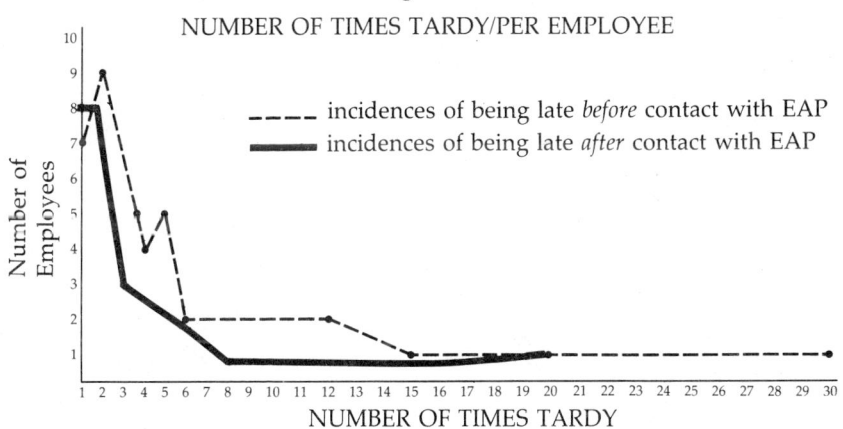

|  | Number of Times Arriving Late | |
|---|---|---|
|  | Before contact with the EAP | After contact |
| Mean (average) | 5.0 | 2.9 |
| Mode (most common) | 2.0 | 1 & 2 |
| Median (middle) | 15.0 | 10.0 |
| Range | 1–30 | 1–20 |

# APPENDIX TWO
# SUMMARIES OF SELECTED STUDIES

# SUMMARIES OF SELECTED STUDIES

It should be pointed out that this review is not intended to be exhaustive and detailed, but rather focused on those studies most relevant to research and evaluation needs. Our aim is to provide information on broadbrush EAPs and the evaluation of them. However, because much of the research on EAPs has focused on alcohol-only programs, we include them as well. Researchers interested in a more thorough review of the literature can find excellent ones elsewhere (Trice, 1980).

## Table 17
### CHARACTERISTICS OF TROUBLED EMPLOYEES

| Source | Sample Characteristics | Criteria | Findings |
|---|---|---|---|
| Schramm, 1977 | Problem drinkers | Absenteeism | Absenteeism rate of problem drinkers 1 year prior to intervention exceeded the company rate by as much as 8 times. |
| Saad & Madden, 1976 | 73 alcoholic men | Absenteeism | Average yearly loss was 86.1 days; for men in general in that geographical area (NW England) average was 19.8. |
| Cole & Shope, 1970 | 32 schizophrenics & 75 psychoneurotics & controls (healthy employees) | Promotions | Controls received more promotions than schizophrenics (47% vs. 29%). |
| | | Turnover rate | Turnover rate for schizophrenics and psychoneurotics was roughly twice that of controls. |
| | | Work Performance Inventory (objective ratings) | No difference between emotionally disturbed and control groups. |
| | | Absenteeism over 1 year | Psychoneurotics were absent more than controls (77 days vs. 47 days). Schizophrenic group also had higher absenteeism rate than controls. |
| | | Medical visits | No differences. |
| | | On-the-job injuries | No differences. |

| | | | |
|---|---|---|---|
| Kurtz, et al., 1980 | 39 EAP clients from a large public utility | Self-report of drinking problems | Clients reported a mean of 4.9 years of problem drinking prior to referral. |
| | | Self-report of work performance | 24/39 felt their drinking interfered with their job performance. |
| Mannello, 1979 | 1571 problem drinkers from 7 railroads | Absenteeism | Problem drinkers were absent about twice as often as non-problem drinkers. |
| | | Productivity (supervisor's ratings) | Problem drinkers estimated by supervisors to work at 50% of potential; non-problem drinkers estimated to work at 70% of their potential. |
| Schramm et al., 1978 | 206 EAP referrals (alcohol problems) 100 non-alcoholics | Job tenure | Median job tenure for EAP clients was 10 years, with 53% working on the same job 10 years or more. Comparison group (non-alcoholics) had median job tenure of 20 years, with 76% on the same job for 10 years or more. |
| | | Social stability scale (measure of number of changes in living situation, job, in past 5 years) | EAP clients had much less social stability than comparison group (36% of the EAP clients vs. 85% of comparison group scored high on social stability scale). |

## Table 18
## CLIENT OUTCOME STUDIES

| Source | Type of Company | Sample Characteristics(N) | Type of EAP | Type of Treatment | Length of Follow-up | Criteria | Outcome |
|---|---|---|---|---|---|---|---|
| Heyman, 1976 | 4 large service and manufacturing | 162 | alcoholism | | | Self-reported work performance | 67% of coerced clients and 33% of voluntary clients improved |
| Manello, 1979 | 7 railroads | 1,571 | alcoholism | | | "return to adequate work levels" | "about 70% of those who accepted treatment were successfully rehabilitated" |
| Milstead-O'Keefe, 1980 | 10 companies in community Agency of Labor Management | 13 women alcoholics | broadbrush | | | 5 measures of work performance | success rate equalled "71-88% across the work performance criteria" |
| Presnall, 1980 | not given | 167 problem drinking men | alcoholism | | | amount of drinking absenteeism | 73/167 improved, decrease from 47-61 work shifts lost annually prior to treatment to 12-21 work shifts lost annually after treatment, depending on drinking outcome |
| Foote, et al., 1978 | 4 companies | Company A: $N=343$ Company B: $N=22$ Company C: $N=57$ Company D: $N=159$ mainly men | broadbrush | | 13 months after referral | absenteeism | Company A: no data; Company B: increase from 244 to 298 average hours annually; Company C: decrease from 307 to 133; Company D: decrease from 628 to 492 |

| Study | | Sample | Problem | Treatment | Follow-up | Outcome Measures | Results |
|---|---|---|---|---|---|---|---|
| Chopra et al., 1979 | not given | 86 coerced clients and 100 voluntary clients (all men) | alcoholism | 3 wk. in-patient program | Max. of 14 months | disciplines | Company A: decrease from .6 to .5 average number annually; Company B: decrease from 1.1 to .7; Company C: decrease from 1.0 to .2; Company D: decrease from 1.6 to .7 |
| | | | | | | grievances | Company A: no data; Company B: decrease from .2 to 0 average number annually; Company C: decrease from .1 to 0; Company D: decrease from 1.4 to .9 |
| | | | | | | on-the-job accidents | Company A: decrease from 2.3 to 1.7 average number annually; Company B: decrease from 1 to .9; Company C: decrease from .3 to 0; Company D: no data |
| | | | | | | visits to medical unit | Company A: decrease from 7.3 to 5.9 average number annually; Company B: increase from 12.? to 14.1; Company C: decrease from 2.6 to .?; Company D: no data |
| | | | | | | amount paid in worker's compensation benefits | Company A: decrease from $163 to $124 average annually; Company B: decrease from $320 to $237; Company C: decrease from $130 to $5 |
| | | | | | | amount paid in sickness & accident benefits | Company A: increase from $425 to $679 average annually; Company B: increase from $123 to $205; Company C: decrease from $2035 to $824; Company D: increase from $593 to $629 |
| | | | | | | abstinence | 48% of coerced and 34% of voluntary clients reported abstinence |

Table 18 Continued

| Source | Type of Company | Sample Characteristics(N) | Type of EAP | Type of Treatment | Length of Follow-up | Criteria | Outcome |
|---|---|---|---|---|---|---|---|
| Freedberg & Johnson, 1980 | 200 businesses & industries | 370 coerced clients and 58 voluntary clients (95% men) | alcoholism | 3 week in-patient program followed by 80–90 hours of aftercare | 12 months | abstinence | 31% of coerced and 36% of voluntary clients reported abstinence; 32% & 21% reported improvement |
| | | | | | | work status | 15% of coerced and 7% of voluntary were fired |
| | | | | | | Ontario Problem Assessment Battery | "significant improvement" |
| | | | | | | Supervisor's Rating Form | "significant improvement" |
| Anonymous, 1980 | Illinois Bell | 752 referred problem drinkers with at least 5 years of employment before and after referral | alcoholism | varied; hospital recommended for 50% | at least one year | abstinence | 58% reported abstinence; 19% reported improvement |
| | | | | | | supervisor's ratings | prior to referral 90% had fair to poor ratings after referral 66% had good ratings |
| | | | | | | disability claims | decreased by 52% |
| | | | | | | off-duty accidents requiring > 7 day absence | decreased by 42.4% |
| | | | | | | on-duty accidents | decreased by 61.4% |
| Schramm, et al., 1978 | 3 companies | 205 referred problem drinkers | alcoholism | varied; in-patient recommended for 10% | 3–30 months | job retention | 83.3% remained employed in the company |
| | | | | | 12–30 months | treatment outcome | 38.3% successfully completed treatment or were still actively involved in treatment |

Table 19

## HAZELDEN CLIENT OUTCOME STUDIES

| Source | Sample Type of Company | Charac- teristics | Type of EAP | Type of Treatment | Length of Follow-up | Criteria | Outcome |
|---|---|---|---|---|---|---|---|
| Spicer, Barnett, & Kliner, 1979 | Referrals from many companies to a treatment center. (Hazelden) | N = 191 (Mostly males) | N/A | 4 week residential treatment | 12 Months | Self-reported alcohol use. | 69% abstinent (compared with 62% in total patient population) |
| | | | | | | Self-reported drug use. | 78% abstinent (compared with 70% in total patient population) |
| | | | | | | Self-reported improvement in: relationship with spouse, general physical health, self-image, ability to manage finances. | 78–91% reported improvement |
| | | | | | | Self-reported improvement in job performance. | 85% reported improvement |
| | | | | | | A.A. attendance ≥ 1 × week. | 58% reported improvement |
| | | | | | | Self-reported improvement in overall quality of life. | 59% reported improvement |
| | | | | | | Self-reported: | |
| | | | | | | quality of work | 46% improved |
| | | | | | | quantity of work | 35% improved |
| | | | | | | relationship with co-workers | 33% improved |
| | | | | | | relationship with supervisors | 32% improved |
| | | | | | | # of times arrived to work late | Decrease from 196 times to 61 times total |
| | | | | | | # of times left work early | Decrease from 120 times to 43 times |
| Hazelden, 1981 | Hennepin County Employees | N = 109 EAP Clients 63% women 37% men | broadbrush | Varied; only 48% referred to inpatient treatment | 4 Months | # of times other absenteeism | Decrease from 56 times to 0 times |
| | | | | | | Times used health insurance plan | Decrease from 96 to 90 |
| | | | | | | Sick days | Decrease from 158 to 126 |
| | | | | | | Medical leave days | Increase from 41 to 75 |
| | | | | | | Accidents on job | No change (2) |
| | | | | | | Times used Workers' Compensation | Decrease from 8 to 0 |
| | | | | | | Short-term disability | No change (0) |

## Table 20
## COST-BENEFIT OUTCOMES

| Source | Type of Company | Formulas Used | Cost-Benefit Outcome |
|---|---|---|---|
| Foote et al., 1978 | 4 companies ($N = 581$) | 1 day absent = 1 day employee's wages<br>1 accident = 1 hour employee's wages<br>1 medical unit visit = 1 hour employee's wages<br>1 disciplinary action = 3 hours employee's wages<br>1 grievance = 5 hours employee's wages<br>(Each of the above adjusted according to rates in the general company population.) | Absenteeism is the largest cost factor. Cost-savings per client for absenteeism was estimated to be $359.95 in in Company B; $1304.30 for Company C; $1196.32 for Company D. (Dollar amounts for all other factors also provided in the report.) |
| Mannello, 1979 | 7 railroads ($N = 28,300?$) | Cost of absenteeism:<br>Percent of problem drinkers in the work place multiplied by number of days absent. Dollar figure arrived at by multiplying number of "man years" absent by average annual salary of $18,000. | It is estimated that the railroad loses over $3 million/year through excessive absenteeism. |
| | | Cost of lost productivity:<br>Supervisory estimate of reduced productivity of problem drinking workers (20%) multiplied by number of problem drinkers (28,000) to compute number of "man years" lost. Dollar figures arrived at by multiplying man-years times average annual salary ($18,000). | Cost of lost productivity equals over $100 million/year. |
| | | Cost of injuries:<br>Percent of alcohol-related injuries (4%) times amount of total disability claims ($12.5 million). | Cost of injuries equals $500,000/year. |
| | | Cost of accidents:<br>Estimate of percent of alcohol-caused accidents (1%) times total cost of all damage due to accidents. | Cost of accidents equals $650,000/year. |

| Study | Sample | Formula | Results |
|---|---|---|---|
| Presnall, 1980 | Not given ($N = 117$) | Cost of illness: Cost of budget of EAP ($1 million) plus cost of premiums paid by insurance companies for alcohol-related cases (2.3 million). Cost of grievance procedure: Formula not given. Cost of rehabilitation: Formula not given. | Health costs to the companies equals $3.3 million/year. Grievance procedures for alcohol cost $408,000/year (or $1,050/dismissed employee). Rehabilitation cost $840 per rehabilitated worker. |
| Marsh, 19— | University employees ($N = 31$) | Based on assumption that each alcoholic employee costs the company 25% of his/her salary per year in absenteeism, tardiness, poor work, etc. and cost of each non-alcoholic troubled employee equals 12.5% of his/her salary. | "Without rehabilitation, each alcoholic will cost the company $500 annually in overtime, extra supervisor work, and extra clerical work." Rehabilitation of clients saved the university $45,000/year (or $971 per troubled employee). |
| Anonymous, 1974 | Oldsmobile Co. | Number of total hours absent by clients with alcohol/drug problems multiplied by $8 (hourly wage). | Prior to rehabilitation, absenteeism cost company $463,520; after rehabilitation, absenteeism cost $237,176. |
| Anonymous, 1975 | Philadelphia Fire Department ($N = 77$) | Not given | Cost for rehabilitating problem drinking employees equaled $27,747 in sick leave and $23,716 for counseling. Benefits = savings to date ($22,931) + annual expected savings ($17,565). |
| Anonymous, 1975 | Philadelphia Police Department ($N = 170$) | Not given | Costs for rehabilitating problem drinking employees equaled $68,431 in sick leave and $50,660 for counseling. Benefits = savings to date ($139,949) + annual expected savings ($60,094). |
| Schramm, 1977 | 3 companies ($N = 206$) | Average number of hours absent (annual) prior to referral minus average number of hours absent after referral minus average annual hours absent by population at risk multiplied by average hourly wage. | Value of reduction in absenteeism equals $586.42 per worker referred. |